LIGHT FOR THE WAY

LIGHT
FOR THE WAY

A GUIDE TO PASTORAL COUNSELING

KATHY ANN CAMARILLO

XULON PRESS

Xulon Press
2301 Lucien Way #415
Maitland, FL 32751
407.339.4217
www.xulonpress.com

Unless otherwise indicated, Scripture quotations used in this study are from the Holy Bible, New American Standard Bible 1995 Update, ©1986, 1995. Used by permission of the Lockman Foundation.

Printed in the United States of America.

ISBN-13: 978-1-54565-751-5

This book is dedicated to the men and women who have tirelessly served with me in the pastoral counseling ministry, sharing with countless thousands the hope there is in a relationship with Christ.

———————————————————

Table of Contents

Introduction

A disturbing trend has manifested in those influenced by today's culture. A brand of theology foreign to what was once considered traditional morality, or common decency, is being accepted without question. Behaviors and attitudes that shocked generations past, no longer seem to. Many have become desensitized to what was once considered common decency and have adopted a sense of amorality that is shaping a worldview of uncommon decency.

The media wields its powerful influence with laser-like precision targeting the young and old alike, persuading with messages that desensitize to the sacredness of sex, the uniqueness of human sexuality, and the relevance of biblical principles. Principles of kindness, generosity, and acceptance are dismissed as naive or immature.

Prime-time television invites entertainment into your living room that vilifies Christian values and glorifies decadence. Vulgarity is presented as the language of the cleaver and witty, desensitizing the captivated viewer. These practices inform a sense of morality shaped by cultural, rather than biblical, authority.

Today's Christian leader has the privilege and the responsibility to address this matter with courage and conviction. Empowered with the boldness and tenacity the Holy Spirit provides, he or she must be willing to step in and teach biblical truth that will build a foundation, transform thinking, and shift perspectives to biblical truth lived out in loving relationships with one another and the one true God.

The pastoral counselor must embrace their role as a Christian leader and take the risks necessary to engage in a dialogue that may include uncomfortable and unfamiliar topics. Failing to do so facilitates complacency that leads to sins of omission. Every Christian leader and pastoral counselor must find their voice, stand firm in biblical truth, and build a relationship of acceptance without extending approval, never compromising God's truth or the relevancy of Scripture.

Pastoral counseling provides the opportunity to speak biblical truth into the lives of those who are hurting, confused, and hopeless. An effective pastoral counselor can shed light on moral choices that have led to shattered lives and teach the biblical principles necessary to equip individuals to make better choices in the future. The effective pastoral counselor must do more than solve the problem or help pick up the pieces. The effective pastoral counselor must provide the opportunity for the individual to build a "sold-out" love affair with God, a relationship where God is central and biblical authority is the indisputable truth. The only true motivation for lasting life-change springs from this relationship.

Five Essentials for Pastoral Counseling

There are five essentials for pastoral counseling.

The first essential for pastoral counseling is that **effective counseling begins in the heart of the counselor**. The counselor must recognize that he or she cannot give to others what he or she does not possess. The heart of the counselor must be completely surrendered to God and committed to absolute obedience to his Word. The mind of the counselor must be filled with the knowledge of God, his attributes, character, and, most importantly, his Word. The effective counselor must be committed to life-long learning, spiritual formation, and the practice of good spiritual disciplines. The effective counselor must live these principles out consistently, with integrity, in every area of their life.

The second essential for pastoral counseling is **discipleship**. Essential to effective pastoral counseling is the process and practice of discipleship. The counselor must meet the counselee where they are and walk with them, demonstrating the love of Jesus, encouraging them to grow in their faith, and allowing biblical truth to inform their choices.

The third essential for pastoral counseling is **evangelism**. Pastoral counseling provides the opportunity for evangelism. Many non-believers come for counseling. The counselor must seize the divine appointments God provides to share the gospel and invite counselees into a relationship with God, knowing that it is only in right relationship with the Lord that true, sustainable life change will occur.

The fourth essential is **reliance on the Holy Spirit**. Complete reliance on the Holy Spirit is essential for a pastoral counselor to be a useful tool in God's hand. The counselor must let his or her weakness be perfected in God's power (2 Corinthians 12:9). Every counselor must recognize their limitations and God's endless supply.

The fifth essential is **the practice of self-care**. The effective counselor must run the race with endurance. The counselor must set aside all that hinders in order to ensure going the distance while serving in ministry, responding in obedience to the call God has placed on their life. The effective counselor must learn about the risk for "compassion fatigue" and practice good self-care — spiritually, emotionally, psychologically, and physically.

Each of these five essentials is of equal importance and must not be subordinated one to the other or responded to in a predetermined hierarchy. The effective pastoral counselor must commit to each of these five essentials in order to provide good counsel that facilitates positive life change and brings glory to God.

CHAPTER ONE

Effective Counsel Begins in the Heart of the Counselor

G ood pastoral counsel begins with the individual who lives a balanced life that demonstrates spiritual maturity and commitment to spiritual formation. Wise counsel springs from the heart of the person who is spiritually mature and motivated by his or her love for God.

"The ministry of care must arise from a servant heart—
the heart of compassion and care."[1]

Effective counsel begins in the counselor who recognizes that he or she must minister from a heart of compassion.

So, as those who have been chosen of God, holy and beloved, put on a heart of compassion, kindness, humility, gentleness and patience. Colossians 3:12

To be equipped to bear the burdens of those who seek counsel, the counselor must first be made, like Jesus, a fit burden-bearer, remembering he or she is doing God's work *with* him, *for* him, and *through* him. Apart from God nothing will be accomplished.

If you abide in Me, and My words abide in you, ask whatever you wish,
and it will be done for you. John 15:7

When there is a lack of spiritual, emotional, and physical well-being, the counselor is "running on empty," and has nothing to give. In this state there is a lack of ability to show compassion to others, and a loss of effectiveness in providing wise counsel. The counselor cannot give to others what he or she does not possess. The counselor committed to spiritual maturity will bear good fruit.

The counselor must commit to spiritual growth and spiritual maturity. Spiritual growth doesn't happen by accident. The counselor must be intentional in the pursuit of spiritual growth to ensure spiritual wellbeing and the strength necessary to go the distance. Developing an awareness of the need for spiritual growth and committing to the pursuit of habits that promote growth is essential for the wellbeing of the pastoral counselor.

"The formula for developing awareness begins with each individual taking responsibility for their spiritual formation and growth."[2]

The practice of spiritual disciplines must be central to every believer's experience of Christianity. It's a practice that takes the believer beyond surface living into the depths, urging him or her to dive beneath the surface of a seemingly shallow world. The practice of good spiritual disciplines is critical to experiencing God's peace and healing presence and will help to equip the counselor for the work to be done.

The practice of spiritual disciplines involves the body, mind and soul. It engages the senses in ways that manifest in a closer walk with the Lord and an expression of faith that is integral, consistently impacting the individual's character, attitude, and behavior.

The practice of spiritual disciplines must be intentional, starting with an awareness of what spiritual disciplines are. The practice of spiritual disciplines must be lived with a commitment that persuades the counselor to not only adopt the practices but to demonstrate them in their daily, weekly, and monthly regimen.

In his book *Celebration of Discipline,* Richard Foster describes three types of spiritual disciplines: inward, outward, and corporate.[3]

The inward spiritual disciplines are described as meditation, prayer, fasting, and study.

Prayer must be central in every believer's daily life. The discipline of prayer refers to conversations with God involving the heart, mind, and soul. Prayer can be a quick sentence or two or a lengthy dialogue with God that spans a generous amount of time. There is no one way to pray or one posture to assume. Prayer can be done from many different postures, from prostrate on the floor, to bended knee, to simple daily activities like walking or driving. Our heavenly Father longs to be near and hear from each of his children. Prayer facilitates this powerful interaction.

Meditation can be expressed through the practice of contemplative prayer, or the act of loving God through adoration. The Contemplative Tradition is one of many ways to engage in communication with God. It is developing and maintaining a sacred romance with God. An act of contemplative prayer is not self-actualization or spiritual self-absorption; instead, it is a conscious effort to connect the soul with God in a way that engages every fiber of the individual's being. Learning the discipline of contemplative prayer can have a transformative effect on the believer's experience of the presence of God.

Fasting is a discipline with powerful effect that involves the body and the mind. Making the choice to fast requires focused attention. This practice of fasting is one that followers of Christ have been doing for centuries.

There are various types of fasts, from abstinence of all food for several days to the elimination of certain foods for a shorter period of time. Fasting from specific activities can also be included in this spiritual discipline. The awareness of deprivation, or absence of food or activity, serves as a reminder to the participant to focus their attention on God. It is important for the individual to discover what type of fast might be appropriate for their particular circumstance or station in life.

The outward spiritual disciplines as defined by Foster are simplicity, solitude, submission, and service.

The discipline of **simplicity** involves good stewardship of time, space, and resources. Priorities are clear, space is de-cluttered, and activities are purposeful and productive. Re-ordering one's thought-life, environment, and schedule can positively impact the amount of time available to spend with God, self, and others.

The discipline of **solitude** is key to physical, mental, emotional, and spiritual wellbeing. Many things compete for precious time, attention, and resources. Careful attention must be paid to avoid the pitfalls of being distracted by lesser pursuits. Jesus frequently modeled the discipline of solitude. The gospels are replete with stories of occasions where Jesus took time away from the apostles and the demands of the crowd. Jesus made time to be with his Father to refocus, refuel and refresh. The wise counselor will follow the lead of the Master.

The spiritual discipline of **submission** requires full surrender to the authority of God's Word and absolute obedience to its precepts. Rather than allow experience, education, or the influences of culture to dictate the content of pastoral counsel, complete authority must be given to the Word of God. God's Word is relevant and provides every contemporary reference necessary for the provision of wise counsel.

All Scripture is inspired by God and profitable for teaching, for reproof, for correction, for training in righteousness; so that the man of God maybe adequate, equipped for every good work. 2 Timothy 3:16, 17

The spiritual discipline of **service** requires loving one another through the expression of the gifts and talents with which the individual has been blessed. Service is about helpful activity that requires giving way to the needs of another. The spiritual discipline of service can take on a variety of expressions based on the opportunities provided in the believer's personal and ministry circumstances.

Foster next describes the corporate spiritual disciplines as confession, worship, guidance, and celebration.

Confession requires accountability. God knows the heart of man. The confession of sin requires that the sinner acknowledge an offense committed and take responsibility for their action or inaction. Confession requires the sinner to do something about their sin. Sin separates us from God (Isaiah 59:2). Every effort must be made on the part of the believer to eliminate any barriers between them and God. Accountability is key in maintaining the spiritual discipline of confession.

Therefore, confess your sins to one another, and pray
for one another so that you may be healed. The effective
prayer of a righteous man can accomplish much.
James 5:16

The spiritual discipline of **worship** relates to the habit of attending weekly services. It is recommended that the pastoral counselor attend weekly services to participate in worship and fellowship in the body of Christ. Being part of the community of faith helps every believer live the life God has chosen for them.

Corporate worship allows the indwelling of the Holy Spirit to be manifested in the fruit of the Spirit and its natural expression.

The fruit of the Spirit is love, joy, peace, patience,
kindness, goodness, faithfulness, gentleness and
self-control. Galatians 5:22-23a

The spiritual discipline of **guidance** suggests the counselor routinely seek wise counsel. The effective counselor must avoid the "lone ranger" attitude that can distance them from the input of the Holy Spirit and the wisdom of Scripture. No one is exempt from problems and issues that might distract them from giving wise counsel. Seeking guidance is a practice that will equip the counselor to provide wise counsel and go the distance serving in ministry.

Celebration is a necessary spiritual discipline. Taking time to celebrate liberates one from the drudgery of life. Anyone and everyone can enjoy a "serious dose of silly."

A joyful heart is good medicine. Proverbs 17:22

Keeping it light, maintaining a sense of humor, and enjoying the moment helps the counselor maintain balance and ensure wellbeing. Enjoying the simplicity of celebration helps the counselor offset the negative effects of the painful and difficult topics encountered in the counseling process. Humor positively impacts the counselor's state of mind and ability to counsel. In order to counteract the stress of traumatic events encountered in the counseling setting, seek ways to enjoy activities that bring fun and fulfillment into your life.

"Humor's most important psychological function is to jolt us out of our habitual frame of mind and promote new perspectives."[4]

Another important consideration for the pastoral counselor is knowing his or her shape, or gifting, for ministry. It is imperative the counselor knows how God has especially enabled him or her for counseling. Each individual is unique. God created everyone with special gifts, talents, and abilities. It's up to the individual to discover what these gifts are, then refine them and use them to honor God.

For we are His workmanship, created in Christ Jesus for good works, which God prepared beforehand so that we would walk in them. Ephesians 2:10

Author Erik Rees provides an excellent guide to discovering God's plan for each person in his bestselling book *S.H.A.P.E.: Finding and Fulfilling Your Unique Purpose for Life*. Rees defines this unique gifting through the acronym S.H.A.P.E.

The "S" stands for **spiritual gifts**. Rees describes spiritual gifts as a set of special abilities that God gives every individual in order to facilitate the sharing of God's love through service to others.

The "H" stands for **heart**, or the special passions God gives to embolden the individual to glorify him on earth with joy and enthusiasm.

The "A" in S.H.A.P.E. stands for **abilities**. Abilities are described as the unique set of talents God gives the individual at birth with the intention of using them to make an impact for him during his or her lifetime.

The "P" stands for **personality** or the special way God wired the individual to navigate life and fulfill their unique Kingdom Purpose.

The "E" stands for **experiences**. Experience can be both positive and negative, painful and productive. God intends to use every individual's experience to shape their character, serve him and love one another in great ways.[5]

Taking the time to make the discoveries necessary to know your shape for serving is critical to effective ministry. The experience can be freeing, exhilarating, and empowering, providing opportunities to live life with purpose and significance and provide wise, purposeful counseling.

Motivation is key in serving. Serving from the wrong motivations can cause harm to self and others, putting at risk the helper and those he or she is attempting to help. The right motivation starts with love of God, self, and others. The apostle Matthew recorded what Jesus tells us are the two greatest commandments. These two verses from Scripture must inform the counselor's motivation for ministry.

"You shall love the Lord your God with all your heart, and with all your soul, and with all your mind."
Matthew 22:37

"You shall love your neighbor as yourself."
Matthew 22:39

The truth in these verses provides the correct perspective and right motivation for serving. Setting aside one's personal agenda or desire for recognition, power, or income must be integrated into the life and ministry of the effective pastoral counselor. Love for God and others coupled with the passion to share the hope that is found in a relationship with Jesus must be the primary motivation for serving.

Do nothing from selfishness or empty conceit, but with humility of mind let each of you regard one another as more important than himself; do not merely look out for your own personal interests, but also for the interests of others. Philippians 2:3, 4

Hearing God's voice must be common practice for followers of Christ. Learning to recognize God's voice is a practice that comes through the Holy Spirit and the study of Scripture. It is critical for the pastoral counselor to recognize God's voice and keep his or her mind and heart from being distracted by the noise of culture. The antidote to this condition is to saturate one's mind with Scripture.

"If you do not consciously combat these cultural deceptions by saturating your mind with Scripture, your body and soul will be inclined to fall back to their natural, default positions, conforming to the world's standards rather than God's."[6]

Bad, even harmful counsel can result when the counselor fails to take this necessary step. The counselor who listens to God's voice will ensure they do not settle for simply what is good, but discover instead what is best, God's best, for the counselee.

At the foundation of effective counseling is relationship with God, self, and others. This relationship must be firmly established in honesty. The individual must be willing to tell the truth about this critical relationship. The reality of this relationship manifests in the individual's attitudes, practices, behaviors, and beliefs. There must be consistency between thought and action in the counselor's relationship with God, deeply rooted in complete obedience to Scripture. Allowing God's Word to inform choices made in relationships indicates love of self and others. Giving way to the needs of others without doing harm to self speaks of spiritual maturity.

The practices of kindness, generosity, humility, and forgiveness define healthy relationships with others. The practice of self-care and good spiritual disciplines define a healthy relationship with self. Healthy relationships with God, self, and others must be lived out consistently in the life of the spiritually mature individual.

The effective pastoral counselor avoids the perception of inflexibility. He or she is open to input, teachable and willing to make a commitment to life-long learning.

The commitment to life-long learning begins with self-awareness and is sustained with focus and attention. While training Timothy to serve in ministry, the apostle Paul cautioned the young man to exercise self-awareness as he prepared for the work he was about to do, knowing it would safeguard his salvation and that of those who would hear him.

Pay close attention to yourself and to your teaching; persevere in these things, for as you do this you will ensure salvation both for yourself and for those who hear you. 1 Timothy 4:16

The timeless advice from Scripture is applicable today. Those who serve in ministry must be aware of their need for wisdom and intentional in its pursuit. Personal and spiritual growth does not happen by accident. The pursuit of knowledge and wisdom must be accompanied by intentionality. It is critical that every pastoral counselor become aware of resources available to them and put them to good use. It is important that every counselor pursue knowledge, no matter their age or station in life. Taking small steps in the right direction will provide benefits that will bless the counselor and those he or she counsels.

The perception of inflexibility can be detrimental to providing good counsel. Individuals who are rigid and inflexible will often resist input from others and sometimes even the Holy Spirit. An unwillingness to be open to the ideas and experiences of others can limit the counselor's ability to provide sound counsel. Every effort must be made to keep God's Word and the guidance of the Holy Spirit foremost in the counselor's mind as he or she provides wise counsel. God can use others to bring new insights to light. The wise counselor will be open to that input.

Practice authenticity. Rather than being religious, be real. Every effort must be made to be genuine. Avoid pretense and over-used Christian clichés, or being what some might consider "preachy." Keep language simple, direct, and always consistent with God's Word. Even when counseling youth, it is recommended that the counselor avoid the use of slang or colloquialisms. Such language can be offensive, even counter-productive in the counseling process. Negative forms of verbal communication can be off-putting and prevent the good work of discipleship or evangelism from happening. Never compromise your credibility for likeability or generational acceptance. Be conscious of the words used in the counseling setting, taking care to be clear, direct, sincere, respectful, and kind.

To be real, the counselor must recognize that authenticity is risky business. Being yourself requires transparency and genuineness. Counselees can typically sense when the counselor is disingenuous. If the counselor has a problem communicating with a particular counselee or relating to their personality type, it is recommended they seek counsel from a trusted advisor. If the challenge persists it may be best to reassign the individual to another counselor.

When there is not a forthcoming answer to a question presented during a counseling session, be honest. Let the counselee know that you will do the research necessary to find the answer to their question and get back to them. It is better to be honest than pretend you know or give an incorrect or misleading answer. Flexing your muscles as the authority in the room can prove harmful to the counseling process. Avoid abusing the influence you have. Instead, be a good steward of the influence God has given you in the role of lay counselor.

Another key component to the heart of the counselor is integrity. Integrity is defined as "being of sound moral principle."[7] Integrity is about consistency. Integrity is caring more about what God knows to be true of you than what others think. The person who walks in integrity allows their moral code, based in Christian values, to dictate their behavior in every situation—at work, at home or serving in ministry. It is heartbreaking to learn of a follower of Christ who lives a duplicitous life. It is disturbing to learn of reports of mistreatment of spouse or children. It is disappointing to learn of a Christ follower who engages in vulgar conversation at the gym, rude behavior in the supermarket, or a disrespectful attitude at a local restaurant. It is critical the counselor is aware of their visibility in the community and behave accordingly, making every effort to avoid compromising the witness of their ministry, the church, or the gospel of Jesus Christ.

Absolute humility must consume the heart of the counselor and be lived out in ordinary ways. When humility prevails in the heart of the counselor the power of the Holy Spirit permits effective use in the hands of God. To be a useful tool, humility must accompany ability.

———————

"The lesson is one of deep import: the only humility that is really ours is not that which we try to show before God in prayer, but that which we carry with us, and carry out, in our ordinary conduct."[8]

———————

To be an effective tool in God's hand every encumbrance must be set aside.

Walk in a manner worthy of the calling with which you have been called, with all humility and gentleness, with patience, showing tolerance for one another in love, being diligent to preserve the unity of the Spirit in the bond of peace. Ephesians 4:1-3

Many things can encumber those who serve from being an effective in tool in God's hand. Barriers like pride, selfishness, habitual sin, or unforgiveness can prevent the work ordained by God from being done. Obstacles that clutter the path must be cleared away.

He has told you, O man, what is good; and what does the Lord require of you but to do justice, to love kindness, and to walk humbly with your God? Micah 6:8

The counselor's posture must be one of absolute humility and complete reliance on the Holy Spirit. The effective counselor must not worship the idol of self-reliance. Such an attitude can cause harm to self and others. All too often, reliance on one's own experience actually gets in the way of the work God intends in the life of the counselee. They become a barrier to, rather than a conduit of, God's blessings for the counselee.

The counselor must pray the Lord will lead them from a spirit of bondage into a spirit of liberty, transforming self-reliance into complete dependence. From the position of complete dependence, the counselor will come to know God better and his or her counsel will bring the best outcome for the counselee. Nineteenth century South African pastor and writer Andrew Murray wrote,

---

"You must come to be utterly helpless to let God work, and God will work gloriously. It is this that we need if we are indeed to be workers for God."[9]

Self-reliance will not be adequate to the task. In the short run, "luck" might provide a few positive outcomes, but in the long run this will not be so. For wise counsel that produces lasting life change, only complete reliance on the Holy Spirit equips the counselor to facilitate God's work. It is only in complete dependence on the power of the Holy Spirit that the counselor is adequate to the task. The counselor must allow his or her weakness to be perfected in God's power, knowing his grace is all that is needed.

My grace is sufficient for you, for power is perfected in weakness. 2 Corinthians 12:9

Only in complete surrender to God's authority is the counselor an effective tool in God's hand, walking the way he has planned. The wise counselor knows this, lives this, and is able to share these truths with their counselee, equipping them to make wise choices.

Good biblical counsel begins in the heart of the counselor who lives a balanced life, is spiritually mature, and motivated by his or her love for God. The heart of compassion and care must begin in complete surrender to God, and be maintained by the practice of spiritual disciplines, authenticity, and commitment to life-long learning. The pastoral counselor who lives in integrity, humility, and complete surrender to God will be a useful tool in God's hand and facilitate life-changing results in the life of those entrusted to them for counsel.

Questions for Consideration

1. What gifts and talents are unique to you?
2. What is your motivation for serving?
3. Explore the reasons you desire to serve as a pastoral counselor.
4. Do you practice spiritual disciplines? If not, what could help you make these disciplines a daily habit?
5. Name one new spiritual discipline you are willing to try.
6. Are you committed to life-long learning?
7. Commit to one resource to refine, advance, or learn a new skill or ability that will positively impact your ministry.

CHAPTER TWO

Pastoral Counseling Essentials

E very pastoral counselor must understand that the primary goals for pastoral counseling are discipleship and evangelism. Through discipleship and evangelism, God's purposes for his creation come to fruition. Encouraging and equipping those who come for counsel to know, love, and serve help every individual become the man or woman God designed them to be. In turn, becoming the man or woman God designed them to be allows them to experience the joy, peace, and abundance God planned for them.

For those who claim to know the Lord, the counselor must teach the counselee how to take their relationship with Christ to a new level. It is the counselor's role to encourage individuals to draw closer to Christ in order to grow to spiritual maturity.

"...as far as Jesus is concerned salvation without
discipleship is
a stunted form of spirituality."[10]

Discipleship requires the counselor to walk with the counselee, teaching, encouraging and equipping the counselee to be a disciple of Christ.

Go therefore and make disciples of all the nations, baptizing them in the name of the Father and the Son and the Holy Spirit, teaching them to observe all that I commanded you; and lo, I am with you always, even to the end of the age. Matthew 28: 19, 20

Discipleship challenges the counselor to counsel in ways that help the counselee grow in their faith, challenging every thought, choice, and behavior in the context of biblical truth.

"Your mission isn't to manipulate hearts—your mission is to connect, serve, share, grow and pray. The rest is up to God."[11]

The pastoral counselor is in a unique position when someone comes to them for counsel. These individuals are often hurting, confused, or hopeless. In this vulnerable state they are open to what the counselor has to say and look to the counselor for wisdom and sound advice. Each counselor must take this responsibility seriously and do all they can to prepare as they facilitate God's work, covering every counseling session with prayer and complete reliance on the Holy Spirit.

Many non-believers come for counseling. The opportunity for evangelism presents itself in the counseling process. The counselor must seize those opportunities to share the gospel and lead unbelievers to Christ.

Always being ready to make a defense to everyone who asks you to give an account for the hope that is in you.
1 Peter 3:15

The counselor must be ready to simply and directly share the gospel in a manner that provides the opportunity for the counselee to build a "sold-out" love affair with God, knowing the only true motivation for life-change springs from this relationship. The great commission must be central to every counselor's ministry. It is imperative that the counselor seizes the divine appointments God has set before them.

Conduct yourselves with wisdom toward outsiders, making the most of the opportunity. Colossians 4:5

Make it a priority to establish whether or not the counselee has a relationship with God. Care must be taken to tread lightly in the beginning of the relationship with the counselee so as not to be off-putting, or judgmental. A careful approach ensures the opportunity to give an invitation to the counselee to come to Christ at the appropriate time. Rather than focus on the problem presented the counselor must keep discipleship and evangelism at the forefront of the counseling process.

The ultimate authority in pastoral counseling is the Word of God. God's Word is sufficient to inform, guide, and direct. It is as alive and relevant today as it was when it was written. The counselor may not find the exact word in any given translation to fit current vocabulary, but the concept, dilemma, or direction in question can be addressed without hesitation or discrepancy.

All Scripture is inspired by God and profitable for teaching, for reroof, for correction, for training in righteousness. 2 Timothy 3:16

God's Word will not return empty or void. When it is read, studied and applied it pierces the mind, heart, and soul—providing insight and direction for every situation.

For the word of God is living and active and sharper than any two-edged sword, and piercing as far as the division of soul and spirit, of both joints and marrow, and able to judge the thoughts and intentions of the heart. Hebrews 4:12

Pastoral counsel must be provided from the authority of Scripture. It is imperative to study Scripture, along with its cultural context and its life application. Without the influence of Scripture, counsel will be vague, shallow, and meaningless.

The counselor must be careful not to become distracted by contemporary rhetoric or popular moral relativity. A commitment to life-long learning predisposes the counselor to read contemporary literature and study current trends without being influenced by unbiblical principles or values. The wise counselor will be discerning and careful never to disagree with or contradict what God's Word has to say on any given subject. Take the time and find the answers in God's Word specific to the counselee's question, concern, or dilemma.

An important consideration in the counseling process is the discovery of the counselee's thinking style. As the counselor gets to know the counselee they will begin to recognize the individual's patterns of thinking. By default, the counselor's life experiences and relationships influence his or her perception of the counselee. Especial care must be taken to keep an open mind and stay objective as discoveries are made about the counselee and a relationship of trust is built between counselor and counselee.

It is important the counselor have a basic understanding of thinking styles. To be effective in the counseling process the counselor must be able to recognize what factors are influencing the communication style of the counselee and the counselor's perception of the counselee. Expression will be unique to the individual and may fall into one of two general styles of thinking, either fragmented or enmeshed.

When the thinking style of the counselee appears to be enmeshed or intermingled they tend to link events together in ways that can be hurtful or helpful depending on the circumstances. They may tend to keep a record of wrongs that makes it difficult for them to forgive or rebuild trust. On a positive note, this person has an easier time recognizing the cause and effect of their choices and behaviors. They are able to connect the dots of their life experiences in ways that can either facilitate change or prevent growth. Taking time to discover which is so for the counselee will help the counselor determine the best course of action.

An example of a counselee with an enmeshed style of thinking might be a spouse who is having difficulty forgiving after an affair. Their unwillingness is keeping them from rebuilding trust. The event may have taken place decades ago and the counselee still links the spouse's negative behavior with thoughts that prevent forgiveness and the rebuilding of trust. Recognizing this counselee's thinking style helps the counselor find ways to teach them how to let go and trust again. Teaching the counselee to "take every thought captive" (2 Corinthians 10:5), and "renew their minds" (Romans 12:2) establishes the framework for a new perspective that helps the counselee move past the hurtful event and rebuild trust.

The counselee whose thinking style is fragmented often compartmentalizes thoughts or events in ways that keeps them from seeing the inevitable consequences of their choices. This individual often has difficulty with the concept of cause and effect. They tend to isolate events, attitudes, or behaviors failing to see their connection to negative consequences. The positive side of the fragmented or compartmentalized thinking style is the individual is often willing to quickly forgive and move forward when they have been hurt or disappointed in relationships or events in their life.

Each thinking style has both a negative and positive side. One thinking style is not superior to the other. The task of the counselor is to recognize the thinking styles of the counselee and respond accordingly. To provide the best counsel, the counselor must meet the counselee where they are and interact with them in ways that bring about positive results. Recognizing the thinking style of the counselee helps the counselor provide effective counsel.

In communication it is also important to recognize different styles of talk. Talk styles can determine the quality of communication between the counselee and the counselor. Having a better understanding of talk styles can help the counselee achieve positive results in communication.

Talk styles are: small talk, enrichment talk, responsibility talk, and fight talk.

Small talk is the foundation upon which all communication is built. It is the simple dialogue between individuals that asks about the day's events, expressing interest in the little things in a light and non-threatening way. The counselee won't care about what you know until they know how much you care. Small talk facilitates the building of trust between the counselor and counselee. Small talk can improve or mend relationships between spouses, siblings, or friends.

Enrichment talk includes words of affirmation. Enrichment talk acknowledges and encourages character qualities, talents, and achievements. It is a form of genuine praise designed to build up rather than tear down. Words can bless or words can curse. Enrichment talk blesses.

Responsibility talk communicates the details of daily tasks and duties such as who is picking up the kids, taking the car in for service, or paying the bills. Responsibility talk demands the attention of the listener, requiring the speaker to be sure the listener is not distracted or disengaged.

Fight talk is destructive, negative speech with no good intention. It is harmful and can destroy relationships in a few careless moments. Words spoken in anger can tear down a relationship and cause harm that takes time to repair. Patterns of fight talk must be recognized and interrupted before the consequences cause damage beyond repair.

Let no unwholesome word proceed from your mouth, but only such a word as is good for edification according to the need of the moment, so that it will give grace to those who hear. Ephesians 4:29

But I tell you that every careless word that people speak, they shall give an accounting for it in the day of judgment. Matthew 12:36

Conflict management is another area that requires significant attention. Conflict is a natural, neutral, and inevitable part of relationship. Conflict exists among Christians, Church polity, and ministry. How it is handled reflects the faith of those involved. As the counselor develops a better understanding of his or her own theology of conflict they will be better suited to help counselees deal with conflict.

The ability to develop a healthy theology of conflict and the willingness to seek resolution is based in common sense informed by Christian values. In life-affirming, God-honoring conflict management, behaviors align with biblical principles and direct the course of resolution.

"Conflict resolved from a Christian perspective provides redemptive, win/win options. It is based in ethical assertiveness and tempered in the reality that true humility is not helplessness but assertiveness.[12]

Circumstances that lead to conflict cannot always be controlled but responses to them can. Conflict was central to the mission of Jesus. He disrupted the false peace of those around him — in the lives of the disciples, the crowds, the religious leaders, the Romans, and those buying and selling in the temple. He taught that true peacemaking disrupts false peace, even in families (Matthew 10:34–36).

There are five steps toward a comprehensive, Christ-centered conflict management plan. These steps represent a distillation of concepts solidly based in Christian ethic, and biblical truth. The five steps are: Recognition, Reflection, Response, Reconciliation, and Restitution.

How conflict is recognized or defined by the individuals involved will often determine the response to it. Developing a theology of conflict may be a foreign concept to many and is an important step in conflict management. Gaining a better understanding of why conflict is managed in one particular fashion over another requires individuals to question their conflict management style when cooler heads prevail.

Recognizing conflict as a natural, neutral part of relationship often stems from how conflict was viewed in the family of origin. Styles of conflict management vary and include being avoidant, combative, or collaborative.

What was modeled in the family of origin will often determine the conflict management style of the individual. If disagreeing was considered un-Christian or unhealthy, an avoidant attitude may have been the response used to address conflict. Sweeping things under the rug may have led to generations of unresolved issues.

When conflict in the family of origin was addressed in a violent or combative way by authority figures, younger or more vulnerable family members often respond by avoiding conflict at all cost. This attitude and behavior would also be best described as the avoidant style of conflict management.

When conflict in the family of origin was addressed in combative, non-collaborative behaviors such as verbal or physical abuse it can be best described as a combative style of conflict management. In this style of conflict management, the dominant personality directs the conflict to their advantage through the use of aggressive or abusive language and behaviors.

The Christ-centered, partnership approach in conflict management provides creative options and outcomes that honor God and each participant in the conflict. This style of conflict management is best described as collaborative. In collaborative conflict management individuals take responsibility for their part in the conflict and engage in appropriate dialogue to address and resolve the conflict. To facilitate a collaborative approach in conflict management and provide creative options, participants in the conflict must first recognize their individual theology of conflict. Rather than shy away from conflict or react in anger, Christians have a responsibility to behave in a manner reflective of their walk with the Lord. During the initial stage of conflict management, it is important to see the conflict for what it is and be willing to step back and prepare to respond to the conflict in an appropriate manner.

Recognition of conflict starts in the heart of the individuals involved in the conflict. Perception of the event influences the emotional state of the individuals, and while their feelings may be real, they may not reflect reality. Remembering that the heart is often deceitful (Jeremiah 17:9), individuals must begin the process with honesty to God, self, and others. To mitigate conflict and work toward mutually beneficial solutions individuals must be encouraged to frame their theology of conflict in Scripture, and the experience of what they learned about conflict management from their family of origin. Each person must be willing to first come before the Lord and prayerfully ask for the help they need to see the truth of the issues involved in the conflict. How conflict is experienced, evaluated, and defined will determine its resolution.

Recognizing and resolving conflict in a Christ-like manner requires answers to some important questions. Taking the time to discover conflict management style is an important first step. Ask the counselee if they see themselves as avoidant, combative, or collaborative in their style of conflict management. Help them discover which conflict management style describes them and how to prepare for successful conflict resolution. These steps will help set them up to win.

Does the conflict involve a principle, value, personality, or preference? Understanding the context of the conflict helps determine how flexible or willing to compromise an individual will be. Healthy, Christ-centered conflict management does not mean compromising one's primary values or biblical truth.

Prayer can soften the hardest of hearts. Encourage a time of prayer prior to arranging a conflict management session. It is crucial to the outcome of the conflict to hit the pause button and take the time to pray and reflect on the matter apart from the heat of the moment. When this step is overlooked individuals will be tempted to react rather than respond to the conflict.

Encourage participants to search the Bible for God's perspective in the matter. When conflict occurs, it is critical to take time to reframe the incident from a biblical perspective. When taking the first step toward conflict management individuals must exercise self-discipline, tempered in awareness of their conflict management style and willingness to respond in obedience to biblical principles.

After taking the time to pray and adopt a biblical perspective, individuals have the opportunity to choose to put away childish things in order to think and act in a responsible, Christ-like manner.

When I was a child, I used to speak like a child, think like a child, reason like a child; when I became a man, I did away with childish things. 1 Corinthians 13:11

As the parties involved prepare to step into the next phase of conflict management it is important for them to reflect on the situation. Participants must be encouraged to take the time to look into God's Word for guidance, to listen to the Holy Spirit and to seek wise counsel. This step of reflection will help prevent the individuals from reacting inappropriately. Individuals may need to learn new skills before responding to the conflict. Encourage postponing a response until emotions have cooled and effective skills have been learned. Encourage participants to avoid the temptation to respond when emotions are running high.

When learning new skills of conflict management, it is helpful to enlist the support of a prayer partner. A trusted prayer partner is someone to pray with and help search God's Word for a biblical perspective. Participants must be ready and willing to listen to their prayer partner, see the truth when it's presented, and take responsibility for their part in the conflict. Even when they are only 2% responsible, they must take full responsibility for their part.

A Christian ethic of conflict management recognizes the destructive potential of the conflict and provides redemptive, saving options based in humility and ethical assertiveness, the kind of assertiveness that balances self-respect with respect of others.[13]

Once individuals have taken the time to recognize their conflict management style, reflect on the nature of the conflict, and take responsibility for their part, set up a time to respond to the situation. Help the person with an avoidant conflict management style be willing to risk confrontation, the combative to cool down, and the collaborative to seek the best approach. Scripture cautions against unresolved conflict, encouraging instead that each person makes every attempt to be at peace with others.

*If possible, so far as it depends on you, be at peace with
all men.* Romans 12:18

A Christ-like response is tempered in biblical principles and
includes confession.

A Christian ethic of conflict management is based in spiritual and emotional maturity expressed in words that speak the
truth in love and kindness.

A Christian ethic of conflict management is expressed in
words that do no harm.

*A gentle answer turns away wrath, but a harsh word stirs
up anger.* Proverbs 15:1

A Christian ethic of conflict management avoids the use of
absolutes like "always" and "never." It avoids angry outbursts,
the use of profanity or the silent treatment. The individual's
response to the conflict facilitates either a win/win outcome or
causes damage often difficult to repair.

A Christian ethic of conflict management includes an awareness of body language and facial expression. Communicating
unspoken words through facial expression and body language
can have a positive or negative impact on conflict resolution.
Consciousness of facial expressions, whether sad, mad, or glad
can impact the outcome of the negotiation. Participants must
be mindful of both their facial expression and body language,
careful not to present in overtly dominant or submissive posture.

The setting for the conversation is also important. Select a neutral place where none of the parties involved has a natural, "home court" advantage over the other participants in the conflict. To ensure confidentiality and privacy, an ideal location will be private and quiet. Encourage participants not to discuss the conflict before the appointed time.

The next step in the conflict management process is reconciliation. To be reconciled means to be submissive, aligned with, and agreeable. Reconciliation means to bring back into harmony those involved in the conflict. Reconciliation tempers spiritual maturity with emotional maturity and seeks to build up rather than tear down. Reconciliation includes a workable resolve involving an offering of contrition and compromise. Even when the desired outcome is not achieved an attitude of humility must prevail and manifest in a gesture that will lead to peace among the parties involved.

Repentance provides substance to words expressed in reconciliation and often begins with an apology. In Christian conflict resolution healing the relationship takes priority over being right, having your way or winning the argument. Christian conflict resolution requires giving way to the wishes of others for the sake of the relationship, the ministry, and the witness of the gospel without compromising core values or biblical truth.

As the conflict resolution process moves toward reconciliation it will be important to establish some rules of engagement. Have the individuals involved in the conflict state what the issue to be resolved is and what they want to achieve through the resolution of the conflict.

After the statement of the issue have them agree to develop an action plan. An action plan should be specific, relative to the issue, and have measurable results. Participants must then agree to try the action plan, including a specific time to initiate the plan. Once they have had the time to engage in the action plan, meet again to evaluate the results. Make any adjustments necessary to the action plan including providing any resources necessary to help the individuals act on the plan. Help the participants acquire what is necessary to facilitate a good resolve. Remind them that the action plan must be a priority in their schedule and their efforts intentional rather than haphazard.

The next step in the conflict resolution process is restitution. It takes time and specific action to restore a relationship. Restitution may involve tangible or intangible assets. Restitution may include returning an item, repaying a debt or making up for lost time. Restitution often involves rebuilding trust. Trust is not a natural response for someone who has been deeply wounded. A genuine attitude of repentance is acted out in forgiveness and restitution.

"Confession is not ventilation or justification, it is authentic recognition of responsibility of one's acts. Restitution is not a repayment to avoid retaliation, it is a responsive work of making right the relationship between the wrongdoer and the wronged. Reconciliation is not a vertical solution in which the forgiver emerges in a superior position, but a joint process of releasing the past of its pain." [14]

Often parties are not willing to invest the time and effort required to fully restore a relationship. Forgiveness is a key component in restoration. Forgiveness is not forgetting. There are consequences for actions. Forgiveness is a biblical mandate that includes confession, contrition, restitution and reconciliation.

So, as those who have been chosen of God, holy and beloved, put on a heart of compassion, kindness, humility, gentleness and patience; bearing with one another, and forgiving each other, whoever has a complaint against anyone; just as the Lord forgave you, so also should you.
Colossians 3:12, 13

Forgiveness equals freedom. A critical first step on the road to restitution is forgiveness. It can seem a bitter pill to swallow given the circumstances, yet trusting that God knows what is best, it is imperative to understand both the biblical definition and the healing power of forgiveness.

"Unforgiveness is the poison we drink, hoping others will die."[15]

There is evidence to suggest that the power of forgiveness can transform lives. It affects physical, psychological, and spiritual well-being. There has been much written by noted secular physicians, therapists, and authors to support the idea that forgiveness impacts our physical, psychological, and spiritual health. Forgiveness has a positive impact on one's physical body, relieving stress and its bothersome and even fatal symptoms of disease.

Dr. Viktor Frankel, author of *Man's Search for Meaning,* observed death camp survivors whose physical health defied the inhuman conditions under which they existed and attributed their better state of physical health to their attitude. Dr. Frankel described death camp survivors who exercised what he called the last of the human freedoms, "the ability to choose one's attitude in a given set of circumstances."[16]

Victims of more common misfortunes would be wise to imitate the behaviors seen by some in extreme circumstances, such as death camp experiences.

Dr. Bernie Siegel also describes this transformed thinking as turning hatred into energy through love. Change can begin when it is understood that forgiveness is not about the person who has committed the wrong but it is about the person who has been wronged. When the person wronged is willing to forgive it frees them to experience positive emotions, hope, and healing. Dr. Siegel shares testimonies of patients who changed their minds about harboring resentments, or hanging on to grudges only to release the "phenomenal energy that can be liberated by surrendering our negative emotions."[17]

When the person harboring unforgiveness and bitterness realizes they are victimizing themselves with negative emotions they may begin to see the benefits of forgiveness.

Forgiveness has a positive impact on psychological well-being. Findings indicate that a person who is willing to enact the forgiveness process in their relationships is one who will most likely experience relief from symptoms of anxiety, depression, and various character disorders. In recent years scientists and sociologists have begun to remove forgiveness and the act of forgiving from the confines of religion, transforming it into the subject of research. Experienced clinicians have identified forgiveness as an inner process, central to psychotherapy, where the injured person without the request of the other releases those negative feelings and no longer seeks to return hurt. This process has physical, psychological, and emotional benefits.

"Perhaps the greatest benefit of forgiveness is that it is a proactive step on the person's part toward empowerment, self-affirmation, resolution, and moving on."[18]

Sloughing off the dead cells of old resentments and unforgiveness can bring about a fresh, new attitude that will provide room for future growth. Like fruit trees in the orchard, dead limbs must be pruned in order to produce fruit in spring. Weeds must be pulled from the garden or the flowers will not grow. Unforgiveness must be rooted out to enable the cleansing effect of forgiveness and its resulting benefits.

Communities, families, and relationships are sustained by those who are unwilling to rest content with conflict or division and are brave enough to pursue the difficult task of forgiveness and its rewards. Those who are willing to embrace the fear and pain that accompany the truth about the wrong done to them and take proactive steps toward resolution reap the benefits. Taking the first step, engaging the will to win against the emotions that war within, can be a tremendous relief and can set into motion a chain of events that deliver positive, life-affirming consequences.

"Our capacity to choose changes constantly with our practice of life. The longer we continue to make wrong decisions the more our heart hardens; the more often we make the right decision the more our heart softens — or better perhaps, comes alive."[19]

Forgiveness is a practice that embraces truth, engages cognitive abilities, and when the process is willfully manifested in behavior, it has the power to move one from bondage to freedom.

Choosing to forgive heals the psyche, mends the spirit, and equips individuals to better love others. It is a difficult process to be forgiving and forgiven people; it takes time and involves struggle.

As Christians we are called to submit to God out of obedience and to offer forgiveness to those who have wronged us. Obedience must trump emotion. It is very difficult to forgive — sometimes it can seem impossible. In truth, forgiveness can only be done with God's help and the power of the Holy Spirit. When true forgiveness is offered, the impact on the person offering it is profound and undeniable.

Let all bitterness and wrath and anger and clamor and
slander be put away from you, along with all malice.
Ephesians 4:31

Ken Sande writes in his book *The Peacemaker*, "Forgetting is a passive process in which a matter fades from memory merely with the passing of time."[20] Forgiving is an active process; it involves conscious choice and a deliberate course of action. When we decide to forgive someone and stop dwelling on an offense, painful memories usually begin to fade. In true forgiveness the right to keep bringing up the offense is surrendered. The counselee who continues to bring up an offense, and claims they have indeed forgiven the offender, must be reminded that true forgiveness does not allow for this behavior.

Be kind to one another, tender-hearted, forgiving each other, just as God in Christ also has forgiven you.
Ephesians 4:32

When an offense is too serious to overlook and the offender has not yet repented, forgiveness can be approached as a two-stage process.

The first stage is a change in attitude and an understanding of what God requires of his followers. Knowing what God's Word says about forgiveness helps in understanding what forgiveness is. It is a response in which the attitude of the heart is expressed.

Forgiveness begins with a request for a changed heart and the understanding that forgiveness is a commitment made to God.

Forgiveness must be extended even when the person who has done harm has not repented or asked for forgiveness. While forgiveness is mandatory, reconciliation may not always be possible or recommended. Forgiveness does not release the person who committed the wrong from the consequences of their wrongdoing. When the offense is too serious, the offender has not changed, or resuming the relationship would present the risk of harm, reconciliation is not recommended.

When circumstances permit, followers of Christ must seek to maintain a loving and merciful attitude toward those who has offended or harmed them. This requires not dwelling on the incident, seeking revenge or retribution. Instead, it involves praying for the other person and standing ready to pursue complete reconciliation when and if appropriate. This attitude protects one from bitterness and resentment, freeing the individual to experience God's abundant blessings.

Conflict resolved from a Christian perspective provides redemptive, win/win options. Christ-centered conflict management demonstrates the willingness to take the time to recognize conflict as normal, natural, and neutral. When individuals demonstrate Christ-centered conflict management skills they are willing to take the time necessary to respond rather than react impulsively to conflict. Christ-centered conflict management seeks reconciliation, and demonstrates a willingness to make restitution, offer forgiveness, and rebuild relationships.

Pursue the things which make for peace and the building up of one another. Romans 14:19

Balancing the tension between humility and Christian assertiveness, modeled by the master, Jesus Christ, presents challenges to pre-conceived notions of conflict resolution. The ability to develop a healthy theology of conflict and the will-ingness to seek resolution is based in common sense informed by Christian values. In life-affirming, God-honoring conflict management the individual's identity in Christ and alignment with biblical principles will direct the course of resolution.

Questions for Consideration

1. What are the two most important goals in pastoral counseling?
2. What is the primary authority for pastoral counseling?
3. In your own words give a one-sentence definition for the three styles of conflict management:

   Avoidant

   Combative

   Collaborative
4. How would you define your own style of conflict management?

CHAPTER THREE

Counseling Subjects

Marriage

Marriage was God's idea. From the beginning God affirmed that it is not good for man to be alone. So in his infinite wisdom he fashioned a fitting helper.

> *Then the Lord God said, "It is not good for the man to*
> *be alone; I will make him a helper suitable for him."*
>
> Genesis 2:18

It was God's plan for marriage that the relationship be one of exclusivity, priority, and mutual satisfaction. God's intended plan for marriage is that the partners in the relationship become as one, loving and honoring each other to the glory of God. Achieving God's planned purpose for marriage has presented challenges to men and women from the very beginning.

For this cause a man shall leave his father and his mother, and shall be joined to his wife; and they shall become one flesh. Genesis 2:24

Marriage can be difficult; it can also be rewarding. Disobedience to God's Word and selfishness are often at the root of marital discord. Marriage problems brought to the pastoral counselor vary—from disagreement about finances, children, or extended family to infidelity, pornography, or emotional detachment. Careful listening and application of God's principles for marriage can bring about resolve even in the most challenging situations.

Most adults marry, many more than once, even in the body of Christ. The divorce rate among those who marry, as of this writing, is 33%. Barna reports in a recent study that the difference between the rate of divorce among Christians and non-Christians is negligible—both are at 33%. Evangelical Christians fair only slightly better at 26%.[21]

When a couple brings into marriage the unrealistic expectation that their spouse will meet all their needs, they are often disappointed. Only when the individual looks to God first will they find the completion they seek.

"Highly happy couples tend to put God at the center of their marriage and focus on Him, rather than on their marriage or spouse, for fulfillment and happiness."[22]

God's design for marriage works. In failing marriage relationships seldom are both parties willing to honor God with their choices and behaviors. The pastoral counselor will see many who are unhappy, frustrated, and hopeless when they experience unmet expectations, infidelity, neglect, or abuse. God's plan for marriage includes the loss of independence for the individual and the mutual agreement to come together to make the interest of their spouse the priority. Mutual respect and submission are not always an automatic response in the marriage relationship. Scripture provides every guideline necessary for a successful, satisfying marriage.

Marriage is to be held in honor among all, and the marriage bed is to be undefiled; for fornicators and adulterers God will judge. Hebrews 13:4

The timeless principles of Scripture must be taught to those who come for counsel. When counselees are taught biblical principles for marriage and choose to be obedient to God's commands, healthy change will take place. In observance of new ways of relating with God, self, and others, transformative events will occur. Individuals grow to spiritual maturity and marriages saved, leaving a legacy of love that prevails in future generations.

Let the husband fulfill his duty to his wife, and likewise also the wife to her husband. The wife does not have

authority over her own body, but the husband does; and
likewise, also the husband does not have authority over
his own body, but the wife does.
1 Corinthians 7:3-4

To begin the process of effective marriage counseling take the time needed to discover why the couple or individual has come for counseling. Ask probing questions and build a relationship of trust, being careful to give equal time to both parties. One or the other may dominate the conversation. Learn the art of interruption and respectfully encourage each to participate. Ask why they have come for counseling, what they hope to accomplish, and what they believe their marriage will look like when the stated goals are met. Encourage the couple or individual that there is hope for broken marriages when each partner is brought into alignment with God's principles for marriage. Marriage can be an opportunity for holiness, not just happiness.

Sometimes only one partner comes for counseling. When it is safe and feasible, invite the other partner to participate in the counseling process. Be careful when counseling only one partner to not allow that partner to turn the counseling session into a time of berating and belittling the absent party. Encourage the person who is present to work on their own relationship with God, taking the high road rather than blaming everything on their spouse.

Caution must be taken when counseling opposite-sex parties. The counselor must do everything possible to avoid the appearance of impropriety or give false signals to the counselee that may create an unhealthy emotional bond between counselee and counselor.

Take time to discover the history of their relationship and the basic dynamic of their family of origin. Inquire about the history of the relationship as well as the type of marriage they saw modeled in their home growing up.

Discover the counselee's thinking style as discussed in Chapter 1 and recognize the talk style they are most inclined to use. Help the counselee(s) define the issue as one of principle, value, personality, or preference. Ask if they are willing to obey God's principles for marriage even if they see no change in the relationship. Only when the answer to this question is "yes" will the couple experience the best chance for healing and restoration of their marriage. Only when individuals are willing to put God first and obedience to his Word first in their relationship will they experience the success God intends for their marriage. Help the individuals see that God hates divorce and will provide the way when they are willing to pay attention and participate in his plan.

"For I hate divorce," says the Lord. Malachi 2:16

Pastoral counseling does not counsel to divorce. Instead, emphasis is placed on God's mercy, grace, and healing powers.

Divorce is not an option for followers of Christ when there are no biblical grounds. Biblical grounds for divorce include adultery (Matthew 5:31) and abandonment (1 Corinthians 7:10–16).

Even when there are biblical grounds, counseling to reconciliation is recommended over divorce. Counseling to separation with a plan for reconciliation allows miracles to unfold when participants are patient and obedient, trusting the Lord for the best outcome.

When there are biblical grounds for divorce and the couple or individual chooses to divorce, it is often appropriate for the counselor to continue counseling the same-sex spouse to help them through the process. When possible, refer the opposite sex counselee to someone else for counseling. Continuing to counsel the opposite sex spouse can be risky or inappropriate, presenting the danger of temptation or misplaced emotions. Proceed with caution in these matters.

When there is abuse of any kind recommend the individual contact the proper authorities and separate from the perpetrator with a plan for reconciliation. Never advise a spouse to stay in a dangerous situation. In some cases, legal action is recommended to protect the spouse or family from either physical or financial harm. Every case must be evaluated on its specific circumstances. Careful, prayerful consideration must be given on the part of the counselor in every delicate situation. Seek wise counsel should the circumstances be unclear or confusing. Use wisdom and discernment in these matters being careful to honor God, the individuals, and the nudging of the Holy Spirit.

When the counselor senses there is more to the story than what is being told, it is advisable to err on the side of caution rather than look the other way, hoping the perceptions are incorrect.

Have the discussion with the counselee(s) about placing hedges of protection around their marriage. Ask where they draw the line when it comes to interaction with opposite sex relationships. Having clear boundaries in relationship can help prevent the devastating effects of an extra marital affair. Having lunch, dinner, or traveling with a person of the opposite sex may present the risk of temptation, as can connecting online, serving in ministry, even praying together. An informal survey conducted among two hundred men and women attending a 30-week lay counseling training clearly indicated the emotional connection in prayer was significantly different for men than for women. The women surveyed indicated a very high level of intimacy while the men did not.

The conversation about hedges of protection will be helpful to each partner in the marriage providing an opportunity to express any fears, concerns, or expectations previously left unsaid. One spouse may have very different ideas about appropriate boundaries than the other. Be sure each party is allowed full expression of his or her beliefs in this area.

Once the time has been taken to establish a relationship with the counselee(s) and the reason for counseling has been clearly established it will be time to determine goals for the counseling process. Once clear goals have been established set up an action plan with measurable results. Apply the steps outlined in Chapter 4, "Getting Started in the Counseling Process," to define the presenting problem, establish counseling goals and design an action plan.

Use homework assignments to move the counselee forward and to measure their willingness to participate in the counseling process. Participation in the process will be directly related to the success of the counseling sessions.

When counselees are combative or avoidant, use the principles of conflict management to mitigate conflict and move the counselees forward to positive resolve. It may be appropriate to resolve conflict prior to establishing goals and moving forward with an action plan.

Fight talk and combative behaviors can derail any effort to improve a failing marriage. Support every step with scripture and cover it with prayer. It may be helpful to focus on every aspect of biblical love. Help the counselee discover how their love is being expressed to their spouse.

Love is patient, love is kind and is not jealous; love does not brag and is not arrogant, does not act unbecomingly; it does not seek its own, is not provoked, does not take into account a wrong suffered, does not rejoice in unrighteousness, but rejoices with the truth; bears all things, believes all things, hopes all things, endures all things. 1 Corinthians 13:4-8

Parenting

Behold, children are a gift of the Lord, the fruit of the womb is a reward. Psalm 127:3

Parenting must be done from God's perspective and firmly rooted in his Word. Parents must be the authority in their children's lives, teaching their children Christian values, behaviors, and attitudes that will sustain them into adulthood.

Train up a child in the way he should go, even when he is old he will not depart from it. Proverbs 22:6

Parents must give their children roots and wings. Roots in the faith establish a strong foundation and healthy life skills strengthen their wings, equipping them to soar and reach their God-given potential. It is every parent's responsibility to establish boundaries and rules for their household and reinforce them. The rules must be age appropriate, fair, clearly communicated, and consistently enforced. It is better for parents to have few rules they can adhere to and enforce rather than many they cannot.

Raising children is not for the faint of heart. Raising children requires dedication, consistency, and hard work. It is the parent's God-given role to teach their children the principles of civility, respect, honesty, and hard work. Parents do their children no favors when they are raised with a sense of entitlement or disrespectful attitudes towards authority. A child raised without respect for authority will face many difficulties in life, including the negative consequences of failing to follow the rules of law at school, work, and the community.

There will be consequences when a child is raised with an attitude of entitlement based in belief rather than behavior. Children must be taught the cause and effect of right thinking and behavioral choices based in God's Word. While parents are called to love their children unconditionally they must include in this paradigm the reality of discipline for poor behavior and choices. Teaching children the clear parameters of biblical morality from early childhood will prepare them for the inevitable challenges of adolescence and adulthood.

It is imperative that parents agree on the rules. Even when parents "agree to disagree," they must present a united front before the children — otherwise chaos and confusion will be the order of the day. Parents must address topics like privacy, curfew, chores, and bedtime between themselves and respectfully support one another in the enforcement of the agreed to rules and boundaries. The way parents model problem solving, conflict management, and respect for one another will shape the way their children conduct their relationships in every area of life.

Biblical principles of child raising demand that parents be good stewards of the influence they have over their children and conduct themselves in a godly manner. Children raised in a chaotic, undisciplined manner are not equipped to make wise choices and will suffer the consequences.

The instructions Paul gave Timothy concerning leadership are fitting for godly parents who possess Christ-like character lived out in biblical parenting.

Women must likewise be dignified, not malicious gossips, but temperate, faithful in all things. Deacons must be husbands of only one wife, and good managers of their children and their households. 1 Timothy 3:11, 12

Children learn far more from what they see modeled by their parents than what their parents say should be done. Children learn the concept of integrity from parents who model healthy, Christ-like behavior consistently. No parent is perfect, but every parent has the opportunity to be authentic, humble, and committed to obedience to God's Word.

Bless your children with the recognition of who they are in Christ. Whether children are biological, step, or adopted, it is critical to accept and affirm them. There may be seasons in the child's development when their choices or behaviors may be questionable. Love and acceptance must remain unconditional. Acceptance and affirmation do not always equal approval. Communication must be clear and consistent about house rules, boundaries, and expectations.

Rather than look for their genetic imprint on their child, parents must look to see who God has designed them to be.

Acceptance and affirmation are essential in building a strong and confident adult. Balancing the tension between imposing expectations and discovering the child's capabilities and giftedness is every parent's dilemma. Parents must help their children build their character and discover who they are in Christ and how God has shaped them. Rather than impose limitations or unrealistic expectations on children, loving parents will bless their children when they help them discover their unique gifts, talents, and passions. Parents must then provide the resources necessary for the refinement of these skills and abilities, steering the child in positive, God-honoring directions to the future he has designed for them.

Fathers, do not exasperate your children, so that they will not lose heart. Colossians 3:21

Children with limited ability or even disability must be encouraged to recognize and develop their *abilities* to their fullest potential. Parents of special needs children have both the privilege and the responsibility to train up their child to become who God has designed them to be in ways that will bring joy to the child and glory to God. Advise parents to seek help from church-sponsored support groups, community programs, and government resources to fully avail their child of the benefits available.

Words of affirmation are critical in the formation of confidence. Children must learn from their parents how unique and special they are to God and to them just because they are who they are, not because of what they do or how they look. A confident child will grow into a secure adult who will be better equipped to meet the challenges life inevitably brings. A confident child will fare better in an unkind world where harsh words and bullying are often the rule of the day. A confident child will be more willing to take the healthy risks necessary to discover and express their unique gifts and talents. Help counselees learn to teach children that with each fall or failure comes an opportunity to learn and grow. Counsel parents to help their children discover that life's trials, tragedies and traumas do not need to define them. Help parents see how failure and disappointment can develop character rather than destroy the future. Words of affirmation will bless rather than curse and are highly effective parenting tools.

Let no unwholesome word proceed from your mouth, but only such a word as is good for edification according to the need of the moment, so that it will give grace to those who hear. Ephesians 4:29

Meaningful touch is essential. Age and gender appropriate affection are important to the development of healthy self-awareness, personality, and sexuality. Demonstration of affection will change over time, parents must recognize what is fitting for each season in the child's development. Boys and girls who receive healthy, life-affirming verbal and physical affection from opposite sex parents are less likely to pursue inappropriate relationships with others. Promiscuity can often be prevented when parents offer frequent hugs and kisses to their children. Parents must also be careful in establishing clear age appropriate boundaries with their children relative to bathing or sleeping together, avoiding any impropriety or pre-incestuous behavior.

Blended Families

A blended family is defined as a family where an adult with at least one child marries someone with no biological ties to the child. The most critical component in the blended family is the parents. The realistic expectation for the blended family is that parents behave as adults and make their marriage a priority. When the decision is made to marry and join families together, the future husband and wife must take time to develop an awareness of the complexities of the family dynamic they are entering into. They must come to agreement about rules, acceptable behavior, and consequences when rules are broken or inappropriate behaviors acted out. When the rules in the former spouse's home differ from what the couple agrees to in their home, children must be taught to respect and obey the rules in the home. There must be consistency and respect for the rules and clearly communicated consequences for disobedience of these rules.

When these matters have not been clearly communicated and resolved between partners before marriage, it is ill advised to proceed with the wedding. Pre-marital counseling will be helpful in these matters giving the proper amount of time and consideration to creating these important rules of engagement and setting the new family up to experience a joyful union. When decisions about rules, consequences, and acceptable behaviors have not been addressed before marriage there is often stress and conflict once the family is living together. The couple must agree to acceptance and flexibility, doing all they can to make their new family joyful and successful for each member. This is often a tall order and requires focus, dedication, and prayer. Visions of "happily ever after" can fade into the reality of different priorities and parenting styles. Confused, hurting, and doubtful, the couple begins to wonder why they chose to marry.

Often one or the other party brings unresolved anger and hurt from the first marriage into the present marriage. Encourage individual counseling, apart from the couples counseling, for individuals struggling with unresolved issues from a previous marriage or other issues such as trauma or grief. It may even be appropriate to take a break from couples counseling for a season so the individuals can resolve past issues.

When a couple is willing to discover what is behind the fights and submit it to the lordship of Jesus they can begin to change and heal. When they can reconnect with what attracted them to each other in the beginning they can renew hope for a bright future. It is always recommended that the counselor ask the individual or couple what attracted them to each other in the first place. Helping the couple reconnect with the reasons they chose to marry will be helpful in redirecting negative thoughts. When counseling a couple, structure questions that will help the counselee(s) reframe their thoughts in a more positive way.

There is hope! God provides all the answers in his Word and when counselees choose to submit to the authority of God's Word, and are willing to set their emotions aside, they can restore and rebuild their marriage. Marriages perched on a path headed for certain disaster can be turned around when they are rebuilt on God's principles. This can be a huge challenge but one well worth the effort.

Let us not lose heart in doing good, for in due time we shall reap if we do not grow weary. Galatians 6:9

Domestic Violence

Unfortunately, this is a topic the pastoral counselor will have to deal with. Often, there is a conspiracy of silence surrounding this egregious dilemma. Victims of domestic violence are often unwilling to admit to the reality they experience. There are many reasons for this and often the counselor has to "read between the lines" to pick up the clues indicating domestic violence.

Domestic violence includes a range of violent or aggressive behaviors within the home, typically involving the violent abuse of a spouse or partner. Domestic abuse is not limited to the male gender. Unfortunately, many women participate in this harmful behavior. The pastoral counselor must address domestic violence with equal attention whether the perpetrator is male or female.

———————

"Domestic violence constitutes the willful intimidation, assault, battery, sexual assault, or other abusive behavior perpetrated by one family member, household member, or intimate partner against another."[23]

———————

In the 1980s, the women's movement facilitated the beginning of shelters and the need to address domestic violence for the sake of the family. Prior to that time, domestic violence was considered a civil matter, not a criminal matter. It dealt with property issues. Assaulting a family member was a civil matter while assaulting a stranger was considered a criminal matter. Some of the stigma from these attitudes linger to this day.

The 1994 Violence Against Women Act defined offenses as criminal rather than civil, provided financing for training and provision of care. An advocacy program was also created during this initiative. The introduction of this act helped many women find their voice and speak out against the atrocities of domestic violence.

According to the United States Department of Justice, Office on Violence Against Women, the definition of domestic violence is a pattern of abusive behavior in any relationship that is used by one partner to gain or maintain control over another intimate partner. Many forms of abuse, physical, sexual, emotional, economic, and psychological are included in the definition of domestic violence.

Physical abuse is defined as violent behavior inflicted on the victim, including hitting, biting, slapping, battering, shoving, punching, pulling hair, burning, cutting, or pinching. Physical abuse also includes restraining someone in ways that deny freedom of movement, medical treatment, or basic health and hygiene necessities. It also includes forcing drug or alcohol use on someone.

Sexual abuse occurs when the abuser coerces or attempts to coerce the victim into having sexual contact or sexual behavior without the victim's consent. This includes rape, mutilating or harming sexual body parts, forced sex following violence, or verbal abuse of a sexual nature at the victim's expense.

Emotional abuse occurs when the victim's sense of self-worth or self-esteem is invalidated or denigrated. Emotional abuse often takes the form of constant criticism, name-calling, injuring the victim's relationship with his/her children, or interfering with the victim's abilities. While emotional abuse is not considered domestic abuse, it will often escalate to a physical level.

Economic abuse takes place when the abuser makes or tries to make the victim financially reliant. Economic abusers often seek to maintain total control over financial resources, withhold the victim's access to funds, or prohibit the victim from going to school or work.

Psychological abuse involves the abuser invoking fear through intimidation. Psychological abuse often includes threats of physical harm to the victim, the victim's children, family, friends, or the pets. It can involve a threat to destroy property, isolation from loved ones, or prohibition from interaction within the community.

Stalking is a form of abuse that involves persistent, unsolicited forms of attention. It can include following the victim, spying on them, verbally harassing them or showing up at their home or workplace. These acts individually are typically legal, but when any of these behaviors are done continuously, without invitation, it can be considered stalking. Another form of stalking is cyberstalking, which refers to online action or repeated emailing that inflicts substantial emotional distress in the recipient.[24]

Victims sometimes minimize or deny acts of violence against them because of fear, embarrassment or cultural dictates. Sometimes a cultural or generational conspiracy of silence exists, making it difficult for the counselor to discover the truth about an abusive situation. Some victims fail to report domestic violence as they believe the lie that they are somehow at fault. Pastoral counseling can help victims find their voice and break the cycle. Teaching an individual their value in Christ and new skills to address and even mitigate the pattern of domestic violence brings hope and creates a legacy of love and safety for future generations.

Many victims report a repeated pattern in the cycle of abuse. A specific period of time may pass, six months, nine months or a year. The cycle will vary. Often it begins with angry words followed by remorse, and then escalates to threats followed by words that blame or shame the victim. The next step might be throwing items, punching inanimate objects like the wall, or harming a pet. As the cycle escalates the next step will often be restraint, a push or a shove. The violence continues to escalate, often fueled by drugs or alcohol, to blows inflicted with the hand or an object that cause bodily injury. In extreme cases a weapon is brought into the mix, creating life-threatening events.

The cycle of domestic violence often escalates in spite of the perpetrator's remorse or apology leaving the victim confused, fearful, and sometimes resigned to the dangerous pattern. The victim may demonstrate a level of denial that allows them to justify the abuse and cope with their circumstances, failing to see that their life is in danger. As uncomfortable as it might be, the counselor must ask probing questions to discover the depth and breadth of the counselee's experience. If the counselee has come with their spouse, it would be appropriate to meet separately with the individual you suspect is being victimized.

Remember to be aware of same-sex precautions to avoid the appearance of impropriety or opportunity for misinterpretation of your intentions. Inviting another counselor to attend the meeting may be appropriate.

When counseling an individual about domestic violence the first priority is always the victim's safety. Once the individual is safe encourage them to find their voice, acknowledge what is happening, and notify the proper authorities. The counselor can help the victim devise a plan that will ensure the safety of the individual and family members. The counselor can help the individual prepare a checklist of important items to gather such as driver's license, passport, social security numbers, medical history, insurance information, bank information, cash, and medications. Provide a list of community shelters and encourage the counselee to secure safe housing prior to setting the plan in action.

Exposing young children to domestic violence has dire consequences emotionally and psychologically. Children exposed to this trauma can take a lifetime to heal. Many will take the pattern of abuse into their adult relationships perpetuating the cycle of violence. In most states in the United States of America, allowing a child to witness domestic violence is considered child endangerment. It is important the counselor knows the law for their jurisdiction and helps the counselee take appropriate steps to prevent the children from being taken from the home by the authorities. Even when the victim looks the other way, exposing their children to domestic violence, the authorities can remove the children from the home. Caution the victim against this neglectful behavior to avoid its heartbreaking consequences.

Never assume that domestic violence is only a crime against women. Men are also victims of domestic abuse and are often less likely to be forthcoming about what is happening in the home. Domestic violence is an egregious, underreported crime against many. Because domestic violence is not considered a mandated report in many jurisdictions the counselor's primary role is to walk beside the victim and help them find the strength to do what is right to break the cycle of abuse and provide a safe, nurturing environment for themselves and their children.

Hope for the Separated

The pain of separation in marriage can leave an individual feeling as if their soul has been ripped wide open. When this happens, God can fill the space with his grace, mercy, and loving kindness. Separation can open the individual to a closer relationship with God and the discovery of his purpose and plan for their life. Healing, growth, and restoration are available and will take time.

Walking with the individual experiencing the heartbreak of separation requires patience. To help the counselee move forward in this process some basic principles apply.

The pastoral counselor can help the individual recognize the state he or she is in and how to move forward from there.

The counselor can teach the counselee to "let go and let God," waiting on him for his best resolve. The counselee can be encouraged to see they can trust the Lord's provision, unfailing love, and unmerited favor in spite of their circumstances.

During separation, individuals must be encouraged to work on personal issues and their own relationship with God rather than focusing on their spouse or the circumstances that led to separation. Counselees must be taught to pray persistently and expectantly, claim God's promises and take the high road to see God's plan for their marriage. Help the counselee discover their motives and take responsibility for their part in the separation. Whenever possible provide information that will help the counselee get connected to the resources they need during this difficult season. Walk with the counselee, be a purveyor of hope, encouraging them to trust the plans God has for their life, even when circumstances look hopeless. Help the individual build a positive attitude. Ask them to remember God's faithfulness and trust him to get them through this dark valley into a bright future.

Spiritual Warfare

Questions about spiritual warfare often come up in the counseling process. It is imperative that the counselor be prepared to answer these questions with knowledge, awareness, and most importantly, biblical authority. Spiritual warfare is real. Satan's influence is real.

*For our struggle is not against flesh and blood, but
against the rulers, against the powers, against the world
forces of this darkness, against the spiritual forces of
wickedness in the heavenly places. Therefore, take up
the full armor of God, so that you will be able to resist in
the evil day, and having done everything, to stand firm.*
Ephesians 6:12, 13

Understanding the limits to Satan's influence and impact on
the individual's life will create the confidence in Christ necessary to win the battle. Sometimes a counselee will want to be
excused from taking responsibility for their actions, claiming
they were powerless under the influence of Satan. Scripture
states this is not so. It is critical the counselee know the truth.
When we are in Christ, Satan has no jurisdiction.

*You are from God, little children, and have overcome
them; because greater is He who is in you than he who is
in the world.* 1 John 4:4

Satan, the great deceiver, is relentless and persistent in
the pursuit of souls. The careless, distracted, or overwhelmed
individual can fall prey to the influence of the enemy unless
they are careful and intentional in guarding their hearts
and minds.

"Satan, the great deceiver, may be encouraging interest in demon possession in hopes that Christians will become careless about other more subtle forms of influence by the powers of evil."[25]

Help the counselee discover the truth in God's Word and develop the best defense against spiritual warfare.

"First let us realize that a demon cannot dwell in a true Christian's spirit. Through regeneration, the human spirit becomes the home of the Holy Spirit. Indeed, it is because the Holy Spirit is within us that we have discernment concerning the enemy's inroads."[26]

No temptation has overtaken you but such as is common to man; and God is faithful, who will not allow you to be tempted beyond what you are able, but with the temptation will provide the way of escape also, so that you will be able to endure it.
1 Corinthians 10:13

To effectively fight the enemy, individuals must know what they are facing. Strongholds such as uncontrolled thoughts, unmanaged emotions, or unmet expectations can cause an individual to be deceived and fall victim to the powerful influence of spiritual warfare. Allowing uncontrolled thoughts or negative attitudes can compromise the counselee's ability to reason or see reality. Dominated by negative patterns of thinking, uncontrolled thoughts become weapons of self-destruction. The counselor can help the counselee recognize the patterns that have created strongholds in their life and are keeping them from God's peace and promise.

Unmanaged emotions such as fear, loneliness, or depression can also cause the counselee to lose sight of what is true. Unmanaged emotions can cause one to feel hopeless. Fear can be based on false evidence. The counselee might be viewing their circumstances from a negative perspective that keeps them from seeing the truth. A threat might be real or perceived. Help them see the reality of their circumstances. If their fear is based in a real threat, help them discover ways to address or remove the threat. If fear is based in a misperception help them develop positive self-talk to eliminate the patterns of negative thinking. Teach them to renew their mind with Scripture.

When the stronghold is one of loneliness help the counselee discover ways to find and enjoy the company of others. Encourage participation in a ministry, support group, small group Bible study, hobby, or activity that is of interest to them. Ask the counselee to take one small step in the direction of building new relationships. Be sure to follow up and continue the process until a connection has been made.

Unmet expectations can become strongholds. Unmet expectations can include non-acceptance of a station or circumstance in life. Unmet expectations can also involve failing to meet the expectations of others. A parent or significant other might have established a goal the individual is not willing or able to meet. One might not be married when they had hoped to be, or not have children when they expected they would. Unmet expectations can involve career, education, or financial achievements that have fallen short of what was hoped for. Help the counselee balance the tension between accepting God's will and praying persistently for an outcome that is practical, achievable, and consistent with God's plan. All things are possible with God. God's best might not be in alignment with the counselee's unrealistic expectation.

Let no one deceive you with empty words, for because
of these things the wrath of God comes upon the sons of
disobedience. Therefore do not be partakers with them;
for you were formerly darkness, but now you are Light in
the Lord; walk as children of Light.
Ephesians 5:6–8

Encourage the counselee to keep a journal of their thoughts, writing down how many times throughout the day they repeat a negative or unhelpful thought.

God has provided all we need to stand against spiritual warfare. The counselee must be reminded to make every conscious effort to avail themselves of the power of God's promises. To stand firm against the forces of evil the individual must put on the full armor of God.

Stand firm therefore, having girded your loins with truth (with reference to Isaiah 52:7), and having put on the breastplate of righteousness, and having shod your feet with the preparation of the gospel of peace; in addition to all, taking up the shield of faith with which you will be able to extinguish all the flaming arrows of the evil one. And take the helmet of salvation, and the sword of the Spirit, which is the word of God. With all prayer and petition pray at all times in the Spirit, and with this in view, be on the alert with all perseverance and petition for all the saints. Ephesians 6:14-18

When Jesus ascended into heaven after his resurrection, he gave his disciples the gift of the Holy Spirit. This third member of the Trinity offers conviction and correction to the sinner and confidence, counsel, and encouragement to all believers. Remind the counselee that the Holy Spirit is their helper and that through the power of the Holy Spirit infinitely more can be accomplished than by the power of the individual alone. Confidence in Christ and reliance in the Holy Spirit will accomplish great things.

I will ask the Father, and He will give you another Helper,
that He may be with you forever; that is the Spirit of truth,
whom the world cannot receive, because it does not see
Him or know Him, but you know Him because He abides
with you and will be in you. John 14:16, 17

When the counselee blames negative symptoms on the influence of Satan or spiritual warfare, be diligent to observe the symptoms. Negative, even harmful, symptoms to look for would be, hearing voices, delusions, or believing they should do anything that contradicts Scripture. Manifestation of any of these symptoms could be indicative of a psychotic break, drug or alcohol abuse, sleep deprivation, or even severe hormonal imbalance. If after it has been established that the counselee does have a relationship with Christ and is indwelled by the Holy Spirit, but continues to manifest negative symptoms such as hearing voices or having thoughts of harming him- or herself or others, have them call their doctor immediately.

Cultural Influences

See to it that no one takes you captive through philosophy
and empty deception, according to the tradition of men,
according to the elementary principles of the world,
rather than according to Christ. Colossians 2:8

Culture has tremendous impact on the choices and behaviors of many today, presenting a tension between biblical authority and moral relativity. Barna Trends 2017 reports there is a new moral code among Americans that indicates moral truth is more relative than absolute.

"There appears to be a dichotomy at work among practicing Christians in America. Most believe that the Bible is the source of moral norms that transcend a person's culture, and that those moral truths are absolute rather than relative to circumstances. Yet at the same time, solid majorities ascribe to five of the six tenets of the new moral code. Such widespread cognitive dissonance—among both practicing Christians and Americans more generally—is another indicator of the cultural flux Barna researchers have identified through the past two decades. But it also represents an opportunity for leaders and mentors who are prepared to coach people—especially young people—toward deeper wisdom and greater discernment."[27]

Moving the counselee toward greater wisdom and discernment is primary in the pastoral counseling paradigm. Wisdom and relevancy are found in the truth of God's Word. Discipleship and evangelism are facilitated by these key components. Wisdom and discernment become the natural expression of a life lived in a sold-out love affair with Jesus and the indwelling power and counsel of the Holy Spirit.

Faith and culture collide in many areas bringing up uncomfortable topics for the pastoral counselor like homosexuality, same sex attraction, and gender identity. God created us as sexual beings. Scripture informs every believer about sexual behavior.

For this is the will of God, your sanctification; that is, that you abstain from sexual immorality; that each of you possess his own vessel in sanctification and honor, not in lustful passion, like the Gentiles who do not know God.
1 Thessalonians 4:3–5

Many young people are asking questions that are foreign to their parents and previous generations. Questions about sexual attraction, expression, and identification are causing confusion for many.

Shrugging off uncomfortable topics is the easy way out and must not be the option for the pastoral counselor committed to helping the counselee discover God's best for them. The wise pastoral counselor will do the research necessary to obtain a proper understanding of difficult topics and the ability to provide solid, biblically based counsel. Expressing common, simple clichés will fall short in helping the counselee face their dilemma. Often, careless words will send the counselee away, leaving them to face their battles alone, influenced by peers, the media, and most dangerously, the enemy.

Understanding some of the current terminology will help the counselor come along side those who live in the margins of society and provide sensitive care that will equip them to navigate difficult terrain.

Mark Yarhouse offers many key terms and definitions that are helpful in gaining perspective. "Sex is frequently distinguished from gender. Gender is defined as the psychological, social, and cultural aspects of being male or female. Gender identity is defined as how the person experiences themselves as male or female, including how masculine or feminine a person feels. Gender role is the adoption of cultural expectations for maleness or femaleness."[28]

The Diagnostic and Statistical Manual of Mental Disorders, Fifth Edition (DSM-5) changed the term Gender Identity Disorder to Gender Dysphoria to reduce the stigma attached to the word "disorder."[29] Dysphoria, or distress associated with gender incongruence, often leaves the individual feeling isolated, anxious, and depressed. The pastoral counselor must be cautious as they provide counsel to those struggling with gender identity issues. Each case must be carefully evaluated. When appropriate refer the counselee to a medical doctor or licensed professional. Bringing the hope found in a relationship with Christ is the work of the pastoral counselor. Helping the individual heal the relationships they have with God, self, and others based in biblical principles is appropriate care for the person struggling with gender dysphoria.

"As Christians provide care to people in a sociocultural context characterized by ideological and political battles, we need to think about rising above the culture war when providing ministry and meaningful pastoral care and support."[30]

There are many opinions being expressed and claims being made today that are divisive and unhelpful. Denominations are being divided as pastors take Scripture out of context to support their opinions. Rather than enter into the debate inform your counsel with the answer to this question, "What would Jesus do?"

In the book of John, Chapter four, it is recorded what Jesus did in his encounter with the Samaritan woman. Weary from his journey Jesus took a break in Samaria and sat by a well. Counter to Jewish culture Jesus asked the Samaritan woman who was at the well for a drink of water. In a brief conversation Jesus revealed who he was and acknowledged that he knew who she was. Rather than condemn or criticize her lifestyle Jesus helped the woman understand who he was and that she must worship him and share the truth with others, that Jesus was the Messiah. In John Chapter eight, Jesus encounters a woman caught in adultery. He does not condemn her for her sin, instead he tells her to go and sin no more (John 8:11). Jesus did not condone or condemn in either of these cases. Instead he encouraged belief in him and right relationship lived out in faithfulness to his teaching.

All are sinners and fall short in the pursuit of holiness. Jesus meets every sinner where they are, engages them in dialogue, and directs them to the truth and freedom found in relationship with him and obedience to his teaching. The pastoral counselor has both the privilege and the responsibility to stand in the gap with the counselee as they draw closer to God and grow in the knowledge of his Word, keeping the primary goals for counseling, discipleship, and evangelism in mind, never losing sight of the fact that in right relationship with the living God and obedience to his Word, individuals will learn to make choices informed by truth.

And you will know the truth, and the truth will make you free. John 8:32

Pornography

Another common topic in pastoral counseling is pornography. The careless pursuit of pornography causes serious damage to the developing psyches of many young adults and greater destruction to an untold number of marriages. Barna reports "one out of three Americans seek out porn at least once a month."[31] Age, gender, and faith practices influence the use of porn, but it is widespread in the Christian community. In the wake of this destructive practice is a young man accustomed to the practice of self-gratification to pornography who prefers this behavior to sexual relations with his young bride.

Women of all ages report they feel betrayed and insufficient when their spouse's frequent porn sites. A wife confides she had no idea of her husband's secret addiction for decades that eventually explained his lack of attraction to her. He only made the choice to break the stronghold when he discovered his sin had separated him from God.

Counseling those addicted to pornography is challenging and often fails when the person dismisses the idea that this behavior is a problem. Many view pornography as a harmless behavior to gratify their sexual desires, failing to see that choosing this behavior is harmful and destructive. Often, the practice becomes an addiction. The addiction involves choosing a behavior that is harmful to self or others rather than seeking ways to overcome the practice, ultimately choosing the addiction over harm to the relationship.

Complex neurochemistry is involved in the use of pornography, making it difficult to break the cycle. "To understand addiction, you must understand how neurochemistry, childhood trauma, environment, socialization, and spiritual interactions affect brain function. At the core of addiction, you will find an individual who is living a life of bondage, fear, isolation, and shame. Breaking free from addiction begins with the renewing of your mind."[32]

Many good resources are available to help the individual in the fight against this powerful addiction. The pastoral counselor can partner in the endeavor, encouraging the individual to renew their mind in Scripture and the practice of good spiritual disciplines to mitigate this devastating practice. Helping the counselee see the damage pornography is causing to their relationship with God and others takes patience and a solid stand on God's Word.

> *You have heard that it was said, "You shall not commit adultery," but I say to you that everyone who looks at a woman with lust for her has already committed adultery with her in his heart.* Matthew 5:27

Sex outside marriage is another area of concern. Culture has a powerful influence over what is considered moral, immoral, or even amoral, giving new parameters to what might be described as uncommon decency or the gratification of sinful desires.

> *So, I say, live by the Spirit, and you will not gratify the desires of the sinful nature.* Galatians 5:16

A culturally impacted perspective affects views on cohabitation. Barna reports that when they asked Americans about their views on cohabitation the majority of adults (65%) either strongly or somewhat agree it's a good idea to live with one's significant other before marriage.[33]

"Christian morality is being ushered out of our social structures and off the cultural main stage, leaving a vacuum in its place—and broader culture is trying to fill the void."[34]

Sex outside marriage comes up frequently in counseling. When asked about the purpose of sex 63% of the American adults surveyed the most common answer given was "to express intimacy between two people who love each other. Younger adult generations are much less likely to embrace traditional Christian views on sex."[35]

Casual sex, sometimes called "hook-ups," is common even among young Christians. Many fail to see the dangers, physically, emotionally, and spiritually of these encounters. The risk of sexually transmitted disease and the power of both spiritual and emotional connection is lost on the unsuspecting participant in casual trysts.

A young woman reports that she has contracted an incurable sexually transmitted disease after one encounter with a young man who persuaded her to consent to sex. A seminary graduate, recently assigned as associate pastor to a growing church, put his family and role in ministry on line for a sexual encounter with a young woman on the worship team. Another young pastor feels he has lost his call to ministry, failing to see that sexual sin has separated him from God.

The apostle Paul encouraged those who were single to see it as a gift. This idea is not a popular one in today's culture, but Paul's teaching on singleness is worth exploring. Singleness may be for a season or a lifetime. Singleness includes the virgin who never married, the divorced person who has not remarried, and those who have lost a spouse through death. Paul's point is that the gift of singleness is about experiencing the supremacy and sufficiency of a relationship with Christ. The single person is free to participate in ministry in ways the married person cannot.

Unencumbered by the entanglements of marriage the single person can often respond to a need within the body of Christ quickly and with ease. The single person is free to live in full devotion to the Lord during their time of singleness. The idea might be foreign, or even unacceptable to many. Describing singleness as a gift is a perspective worth sharing with the counselee that, once embraced, can free them to experience "undistracted devotion to the Lord," and true joy.

Yet I wish that all men were even as
I myself am. However, each
man has his own gift from God, one in this manner,
and another in that. But I say to the unmarried and to
widows that it is good for them if they remain even as I.
But if they do not have self-control, let them marry; for it
is better to marry than to burn with passion.
1 Corinthians 7:7–9

Encourage the counselee who feels less than complete due to their singleness to realize that with God they have nothing to prove. Help them discover that God loves them unconditionally just as they are. With him and in him they have nothing to prove. Teach them to embrace the gift of singleness and use it to further God's kingdom and bring glory and honor to him.

But I want you to be free from concern. One who is unmarried is concerned about the things of the Lord, how he may please the Lord; but one who is married is concerned about the things of the world, how he may please his wife, and his interests are divided. The woman who is unmarried, and the virgin, is concerned about the things of the Lord, that she may be holy both in body and spirit; but one who is married is concerned about the things of the world, how she may please her husband. This I say for your own benefit; not to put a restraint upon you, but to promote what is appropriate and to secure undistracted devotion to the Lord.
1 Corinthians 7:32–35

Sexual sin and cultural influence capture the hearts of many—believers and unbelievers, old and young, male and female. Believing the lies the enemy and culture tell leaves many confused, discouraged, and distracted from God's best for them.

The list is long, the opportunities plenty for the counselor to speak God's truth into the lives of those impacted by this condition. The counselor must be gentle, swift, and direct in dealing with such matters, unafraid of being viewed as old-fashioned or obsolete in their thinking. Rather than focus on sexual sin, focus instead on the counselee's relationship with Jesus, knowing that in this relationship they will have the power of the Holy Spirit and the opportunity to make informed choices based in love for God rather than the desires of the flesh. It is the pastoral counselor's responsibility to help the counselee grow into a greater relationship with Jesus. It is the Holy Spirit's job to convict and correct. When these roles get confused, the counseling process will most often be interrupted, even terminated. Understand the context from which wise counsel is provided without losing sight of the primary objectives for pastoral counsel, discipleship, and evangelism. Understand your role as a counselor is to be a tool in God's hand. Don't be afraid to speak the truth in love.

Mental Disorders

"A mental illness is a medical condition that disrupts a person's thinking, feeling, mood, ability to relate to others, and daily functioning. Just as diabetes is a disorder of the pancreas, mental illnesses are medical conditions that often result in a diminished capacity for coping with the ordinary demands of life."[36]

Psychology is a soft science. There are no blood tests or x-rays that will accurately diagnose mental illness. In the field of psychology diagnosis is based on report of symptoms. Symptoms are reported by the patient or their loved one and can be exaggerated or understated based on the individual. They are often not an accurate representation of the reality of the patient's behavior or circumstances.

Symptoms associated with mental illness and mood disorders can manifest for a variety of reasons including bereavement, illness, injury, and self-neglect. When the pastoral counselor has ruled out other possible causes and practices good self-care such as diet, exercise, rest, and spiritual disciplines, it is appropriate to consider the possibility of mental illness.

Mental illness is a medical problem where the brain is not working the way it was designed to function. The best course of treatment for mental illness is provided by a medical health professional such as a psychiatrist or psychologist, who can prescribe medication and work with patients in the hospital.

Unfortunately, some Christians (48%) believe that serious mental illness can be overcome through prayer and Bible study alone (35% of Americans agree).[37] While we never want to factor God out of the equation, we must accept the fact that modern medicine provides solutions to mental illness. Mental illness is a treatable medical problem.

In the following pages, brief descriptions will be given of a few of the mental disorders that comprise the continuum of mental illness. The description of symptoms and definition of a few disorders is designed to help the pastoral counselor recognize the spectrum of mental illness in order to be better equipped to provide the right resources and counsel to their counselees. The role of a pastoral counselor is not the role of a medical health professional. A pastoral counselor is not qualified to diagnose, label, or treat mental disorders. Recognizing the spectrum of disorders equips the pastoral counselor to provide effective and appropriate counsel. The spectrum for the severity of mental illness is described as mild, moderate, or severe. It is advised that the pastoral counselor only counsel people with disorders that are considered mild or in remission.

The continuum of mental disorders is broad, ranging from disorders diagnosed in childhood, such as autism or attention-deficit disorder, to cognitive disorders diagnosed in adulthood, such as delirium or dementia. Disorders commonly seen by the pastoral counselor can vary from mild to moderate to severe. Counselees can present with mood, eating, sleeping, impulse-control, gender identity, or personality disorders. More serious psychotic conditions such as bipolar disorders or schizophrenia present the counselor with the challenge of providing the best course of care. It is critical the pastoral counselor conduct their role without risking harm to the counselee.

The pastoral counselor must recognize when a mental disorder is beyond their scope of care and make recommendations to the counselee in order that they may find the best care.

Recognizing the continuum of mental disorders gives the counselor a better perspective to counsel from. The following information is designed to give a broad stroke approach toward this understanding. The pastoral counselor who is equipped with a general knowledge of mental illness is better prepared to advise and counsel based in God's Word and to know when to refer the counselee to a medical health professional.

Mood disorders affect a person's general emotional state. No one can answer with certainty what causes a mood disorder. The Mayo Clinic describes a mood disorder as a general emotional state or mood that is distorted or inconsistent with a person's circumstances. For simplicity sake we will look at a few examples of mood disorders, major depressive disorder and persistent depressive disorder (dysthymia).

A major depressive disorder manifests in prolonged and persistent periods of extreme sadness. It is defined by a collection of symptoms that must appear over a specific period of time. Recognition of the spectrum equips the pastoral counselor to give effective care relative to the counselee's spiritual and relational concerns.

The *Diagnostic and Statistical Manual of Mental Disorders* (DSM-IV TR) criteria for a major depressive disorder are: five or more of the following nine symptoms have been present during the same two-week period.[38]

- A depressed mood most of the day, nearly every day, as indicated by either subjective report or observation made by others.
- Markedly diminished interest or pleasure in all, or almost all, activities most of the day, nearly every day, as indicated by either subjective account or observation made by others.
- Significant weight loss when not dieting, or weight gain, a change of more than 5% of body weight in a month.
- Insomnia or hypersomnia nearly every day. Neither insomnia nor hypersomnia are defined in the guide nor does it define what 'nearly every evening' means.
- Psychomotor agitation or retardation nearly every day, which is observed by others and not merely a subjective report of restlessness or being slowed down.
- Fatigue or loss of energy nearly every day.
- Feelings of worthlessness or excessive or inappropriate guilt, which may be delusional, nearly every day.
- Diminished ability to think or concentrate, or indecisiveness, nearly every day either by subjective account or as observed by others.
- Recurrent thoughts of death, with or without a specific plan, or suicide attempt.

To be officially diagnosed with a major depressive disorder the individual must have at least five of the nine symptoms for two weeks and the symptoms must last nearly all day. Many of the symptoms listed can be brought on by a medical condition, substance abuse, bereavement, or trauma, and must first be ruled out before considering a major depressive disorder. The mood in a major depressive episode is often described by the person as depressed, sad, hopeless, discouraged, or "down in the dumps." The DSM describes the essential feature of a major depressive episode as a period of at least two weeks during which there is either depressed mood, or the loss of interest or pleasure, in nearly all activities. The individual must also experience at least four additional symptoms drawn from the list, including change in appetite or weight, sleep, and psychomotor activity; decreased energy; feelings of worthlessness or guilt; difficulty thinking, concentrating or making decisions; or recurrent thoughts of death, suicidal ideation, plans, or attempts. The symptoms must persist for most of the day, nearly every day, for at least two consecutive weeks. The episode must be accompanied by clinically significant distress or impairment in social, occupational, or other important areas of functioning.[39]

Persistent depressive disorder (dysthymia) is a long-term (chronic) form of depression. A dysthymic disorder is described as a depressed mood for most of the day, for more days than not, as indicated either by subjective account or observation by others, for at least two years. Symptoms of dysthymia are similar to those of major depression, though they tend to be less intense.

The individual with a dysthymic disorder will experience two or more of the following symptoms (while depressed) for a period of at least two years:

- Poor appetite or overeating.
- Insomnia or hypersomnia.
- Low energy or fatigue.
- Low self-esteem.
- Poor concentration or difficulty making decisions.
- Feelings of hopelessness.

Dysthymia, also called dysthymic disorder, is a form of depression. It is less severe than major depression, but usually lasts longer. Many people with this type of depression describe having been depressed as long as they can remember, or they feel they are going in and out of depression all the time. The symptoms of dysthymia are similar to those of major depression but less intense. In both conditions, a person can have a low or irritable mood, a decrease in pleasure, and a loss of energy. They feel relatively unmotivated and disengaged from the world.

A dysthymic disorder affects a person's thoughts, feelings, and behavior, often with negative consequences to their relationships. A dysthymic disorder affects a person's thinking. Their thoughts often turn negative or pessimistic and they find it difficult to concentrate. In this disorder the individual often has feelings of hopelessness, helplessness, or sadness. The disorder often affects behavior, manifesting in poor hygiene, neglect of appearance, or disinterest in sex. It also impacts physical well-being through unhealthy diet, lack of exercise, or poor sleep habits.

A thought problem can be less complex. When there is a thought problem the counselee has experienced prolonged distorted patterns of thinking, or "stinking thinking," that have altered their view of their world. They may experience prolonged, intense, generalized, feelings of non-specific anger, resentment, anxiety, or avoidance that have impacted their moods, feelings, and relationships with others. When a counselee experiences distorted patterns of thinking it is imperative that the pastoral counselor encourage the counselee to take every thought captive and renew their mind with Scripture.

We are destroying speculations and every lofty thing raised up against the knowledge of God, and we are taking every thought captive to the obedience of Christ.
2 Corinthians 10:5

And do not be conformed to this world, but be transformed by the renewing of your mind, so that you may prove what the will of God is, that which is good and acceptable and perfect.
Romans 12:2

More serious mental disorders include schizophrenia and bipolar disorder. Schizophrenia can only be diagnosed based on the report or observation of symptoms. The essential features of schizophrenia are a mixture of characteristic signs and symptoms (both positive and negative) that have been present for a significant portion of time during a one-month period (or for a shorter time if successfully treated), with some signs of the disorder persisting for at least six months. The signs and symptoms of schizophrenia are associated with marked social or occupational dysfunction, best recognized by a medical health professional. Diagnosis of schizophrenia involves the recognition of a constellation of signs and symptoms associated with impaired occupational or social functioning. The range of cognitive and emotional dysfunction includes perception, inferential thinking, language and communication, behavioral monitoring, affect, fluency, and productivity of thought.

The symptoms of schizophrenia fall into two broad categories: positive symptoms and negative symptoms. Positive symptoms are unusual thoughts or sensory perception dealing with physical perceptions, including hallucinations and delusions. A hallucination is something a person sees, hears, smells, or feels that is not real. Delusions are faulty interpretations of the individual's environment or relationships that are not logical. These interpretations are even when the facts do not support their conclusions.

Negative symptoms include a loss or a significant decrease in their ability to initiate social contact, make plans for daily care and activity, speak, express emotion, or initiate activity that brings pleasure or joy in everyday life. Negative symptoms are the absence of normal emotions and behaviors and often include a flat affect and a diminished ability to start and continue planned activity. They may neglect basic hygiene and fail to maintain daily activities such as going to work or caring for children.[40]

Schizophrenia is considered to be the "granddaddy" of mental illness and, when the symptoms are severe, the counselee often needs to be institutionalized for their own welfare. When the symptoms are moderate to mild, the counselee may experience shifting symptoms and, under most circumstances, can function within the far limits of normalcy. When the counselee is on the mild end of the spectrum the pastoral counselor can provide spiritual guidance that can positively impact the schizophrenic's quality of life. Unless the counselee is partnering with their medical health professional and taking their prescribed medication as directed, it is not recommended the pastoral counselor counsel an individual diagnosed with schizophrenia. Supportive counseling for the schizophrenic might include providing counseling for the spouse or a significant loved one.

It is important to note that people with schizophrenia do attempt suicide more often than others. This frequently occurs when the counselee decides to stop taking their medication without consulting with their physician.

All talk of suicide is taken seriously. When working with any counselee who has been diagnosed with a mental illness, be more vigilant in such talk. It is highly recommended that you do not counsel individuals who are diagnosed with moderate to severe schizophrenia.

Another serious mental disorder is bipolar disorder. Bipolar disorder is spread across a continuum from severe to mild. Formerly called manic depression, bipolar disorder causes extreme mood swings that include emotional highs and lows. Bipolar disorder is the dramatic swing in the counselee's mood from one of high elation to one of sadness and hopelessness, then back again.

There are often periods of normal moods between the swings. Mood swings for a counselee diagnosed with bipolar disorder have a negative impact on that individual's ability to control their thoughts and behaviors. The period of high is called a mania episode and a period of low is called a depressive episode. Bipolar disorder is the combination of both mania and depressive episodes. For a person with bipolar disorder, the mania episode lasts for a week or longer and the depressive episode lasts for at least two weeks.

During the severe symptoms of a manic or depressive episode, hospitalization may be required to prevent the individual from harming themselves or others.

During a manic episode the person with bipolar disorder will have an extremely high or energized mood. The elevated mood can also be one of extreme irritability and anger. During a manic episode, the individual can have unrealistic views regarding what they can and cannot do. The counselee generally enjoys the experience of the mania episode and tends to resist any suggestion that something is wrong.

In the manic phase the person with bipolar disorder often engages in excessive use of alcohol, drugs, or sex. When the symptoms of the manic episode are severe, it is likely they will experience psychotic thought. Psychotic thought includes delusions and hallucinations.

In a depressive episode the person with bipolar disorder may manifest the following symptoms:

- A lasting sad, anxious, or empty mood.
- Feelings of hopelessness or pessimism.
- Feelings of guilt, worthlessness, or helplessness.
- Loss of interest or pleasure in activities once enjoyed, including sex.
- Decreased energy, a feeling of fatigue or of being "slowed down."
- Difficulty concentrating, remembering, making decisions.
- Restlessness or irritability.
- Sleep disturbances like insomnia or hyposomnia.
- Changes in appetite or unintended weight loss or gain.
- Thoughts of death or suicide, or suicide attempts.

The symptoms of a depressive episode are similar to those of depression, but also with some major differences. Symptoms may increase due to the reality of what the individual may have done during a manic episode, often leading to a heightened sense of remorse and regret.

The risk of suicide often increases during a depressive episode. It is important for the person with bipolar disorder to learn how to manage their symptoms and prepare for mood swings in order to decrease the risk of suicide.

When counseling a person with mild to moderate bipolar disorder the pastoral counselor must be aware of the counselee's symptoms and mood swings. The individual will typically manifest episodes of mania and depression generally over a period of time. The time between mood swings will vary and most people are free from their symptoms between episodes. A concern is that the counselee can come to believe they are "cured" when they are free of symptoms and do not need to continue seeing their doctor or taking their medication as prescribed. Without treatment the person may suffer more frequent mood swings. When a counselee chooses to stop taking their medication the pastoral counselor must encourage them to follow their doctor's orders. Should the counselee refuse, it is recommended the counseling sessions discontinue.

Another common disorder seen in the lay counseling setting is anxiety. A person with an anxiety disorder often allows fear to control their thoughts, showing signs of excessive, irrational fear and dread. Anxiety disorders can range from panic attacks to specific phobias provoked by specific objects or situations, obsessive-compulsive disorders or posttraumatic stress disorder. Posttraumatic stress disorders are "characterized by the reexperiencing of an extremely traumatic event accompanied by symptoms of increased arousal and by avoidance of stimuli associated with the trauma."[41]

When people with an anxiety disorder experience an anxiety attack there is a chemical reaction in the body. This reaction is called the "fight or flight" response. In this condition the adrenal gland responds to excitement, stress, or perceived threat by secreting a hormone that raises blood pressure, increases heart rate, and heightens the senses to react to the situation. Symptoms may include profuse sweating, trembling, nausea, tightness in the chest, and difficulty breathing.

As the pastoral counselor learns to recognize the various symptoms of anxiety disorders, they must pray for wisdom and discernment as they move forward in the counseling process. Anxiety disorders vary in severity. Some who experience anxiety disorders respond well to spiritual and relational counseling provided in pastoral counseling, while others require the help of a medical health professional. It is appropriate for the pastoral counselor to also seek wise counsel when dealing with an anxiety disorder.

The same symptoms manifest when a person experiences fear. The difference between fear and anxiety is with fear there is a known stimulus, while with anxiety there is no known stimuli. Fear associated with specific stimuli is a phobia. Some phobias are specific to a circumstance or object. "The essential feature of specific phobia is marked and persistent fear of clearly discernable, circumscribed objects or situations. Exposure to the phobic stimulus almost invariably provokes an immediate anxiety response."[42]

Anxiety attacks and phobias are treatable with medication and counseling. Teach relaxation techniques and have the counselee memorize several verses to repeat in preparation for an anxiety attack. Also encourage them to keep a written copy of relaxation techniques as well as Scripture verses with them at all times.

When a person struggles with anxiety they often make decisions based in fear rather than faith. Jesus tells us to be anxious for nothing. Helping the counselee choose faith over fear takes patience and perseverance. God's Word is full of reminders about anxiety.

For this reason I say to you, do not be anxious for your life, as to what you shall eat or what you shall drink; nor for your body, as to what you shall put on. Matthew 6:25

Relaxation techniques are effective in mitigating anxiety attacks. Teaching the counselee a relaxation technique can help them overcome the sometimes debilitating effects of an anxiety attack. The following relaxation technique has proven helpful.

Relaxation technique:

In a seated position, place both feet flat on the floor, arms at your side and hands in your lap. Keep your eyes open during the exercise.

Take a deep breath, in through the nose, hold for a count of ten, then slowly exhale through the mouth. Notice how the chest feels when the muscles are holding the air in, and how it feels when the air is let out through the mouth. Take two more deep breaths, hold for a count of ten, exhale slowly and relax the chest muscles. Notice that as the chest muscles relax, tension is released. With each breath notice how it feels when muscles are tight and when they are relaxed.

Next, press the toes to the floor, hold for a count of five, then slowly relax the muscles in the feet noticing the difference between muscles that are tense and muscles that are relaxed. Press the toes one more time to the floor, hold for a count of five, noticing the difference between tension and relaxation.

Next, tighten the calf muscles, hold them for a count of five, then slowly relax them. While doing this, continue to breathe slowly, in through the nose, out through the mouth. Repeat the exercise, noticing the difference between the tense and relaxed calf muscles.

Next, tighten your thigh muscles; hold for a count of five then slowly relax noticing the difference between feeling tense and feeling relaxed.

Next, tighten the buttocks muscles and hold for a count of five. Notice how much energy it takes to hold these muscles tight, then slowly release the tension and notice how much more pleasant it feels when the muscles are relaxed. Continue to breathe slowly. Repeat the exercise, tightening the buttocks muscles, holding for a count of five, then slowly releasing the tension.

Next, tighten the stomach muscles and hold for a count of five, then slowly relax the stomach muscles, noticing the difference. Take another deep breath, hold for a count of five, and then slowly exhale through the mouth. Notice the difference between how they feel when they are relaxed. Repeat. Next, push the shoulders, hold for a count of five, and then slowly let them relax. Tense and release the shoulders again. Notice how it feels when your chest muscles are tense and when they are relaxed. One more time, tighten your stomach muscles and hold for a count of five, then release.

Next, make a tight fist with the right hand, hold for a count of five, and then slowly relax the fist. Make another fist with your right hand, hold for a count of five then slowly release the tension noticing the difference.

Next, make a tight fist with the left hand, hold for a count of five then slowly relax. Repeat one more time.

Next, take the shoulders and push them back and hold for a count of five, slowly relax the shoulders noticing the difference between how it feels when they are tense and when they are relaxed.

Next, push the lower jaw forward and hold for a count of five. Take your jaw and push it to either side and hold it for a count of five and then slowly relax your jaw.

Finally, wrinkle up your forehead as hard as you can and hold it for a count of five then slowly let your forehead relax, noticing the difference between the tension and how it feels when relaxed. Wrinkle your forehead one more time and then relax it.

Now two deep breathes, in through your nose, hold for a count of five then slowly release through your mouth.

*Be anxious for nothing, but in everything by prayer and
supplication with thanksgiving let your requests be made
known to God. And the peace of God, which surpasses all
comprehension, shall guard your hearts and your minds
in Christ Jesus.* Philippians 4:6-7

Another mental disorder commonly seen in the counseling setting is narcissism. A person with a narcissistic personality disorder has an inflated sense of their own importance, a deep need for admiration, and a lack of empathy for others.

Recognizing the symptoms of a person with a narcissistic personality disorder is helpful when observing irrational behavior and relational difficulties. The narcissist is often extremely selfish and quick tempered. Behind this mask of ultra-confidence lies a fragile self-esteem that is vulnerable to the slightest criticism. This person might be extremely volatile in close personal relationships.

The DSM-5 criteria for narcissistic personality disorder includes the following:

- Having an exaggerated sense of self-importance.
- Expecting to be recognized as superior even without achievements that warrant it.
- Having an exaggerated expression of achievements and talents.
- Preoccupation with fantasies about success, power, brilliance, beauty, or the perfect mate.

- Believing in superiority that can only be understood by, or associated with, equally superior people.
- Requiring constant admiration.
- Having a sense of entitlement.
- Expecting special favors and unquestioning compliance with personal expectations.
- Taking advantage of others to get what is wanted.
- Inability or unwillingness to recognize the needs and feelings of others.
- Being envious of others and believing others envy you.
- Behaving in an arrogant or haughty manner.[43]

In summary, before considering mental illness, determine if the mood is a result of a specific event or circumstance in the person's life such as loss, trauma, medical problem, or substance abuse. Once all other causes have been ruled out, and the pastoral counselor's observations indicate the possibility of mental illness or mood disorder, it is imperative the counselee be referred to a medical health professional for a clear diagnosis. Once a diagnosis has been made, medical health professionals can best treat mental illness and mood disorders. When the diagnosis is mild to moderate and the individual is willing to partner with their doctor and take their medication as prescribed, counseling may be indicated and effective.

Successful outcomes are available to those who take their medication and partner with their physician, or licensed clinical therapist. The pastoral counselor can provide hope and healing from a spiritual and relational perspective. Many with mental illness or mood disorders have caused serious damage to the most important relationships in their lives with spouse, family, friends, and employers. The courage, tenacity, and hope necessary to heal, as well as the strength needed to go the distance in the battle, is found in a relationship with the living God. Healing the damage takes time, patience, and persistence. Walking beside the person who is willing to repair damaged relationships requires consistent encouragement from the Word of God. The challenge to the pastoral counselor is to help the counselee see and believe their weakness is perfected in God's power, and that his grace is sufficient for the task.

My grace is sufficient for you, for power is perfected in weakness. 2 Corinthians 12:9

When counseling a person with a diagnosed mental illness or mood disorder there are recommended guidelines for the pastoral counselor.

Being a pastoral counselor is not about diagnosing, labeling, or defining mental disorders. Recognizing the spectrum of mental disorders is a complex task and helps the counselor determine if pastoral counseling is appropriate for the individual. The pastoral counselor must stay focused and objective to avoid getting caught up in the individual's story. The pastoral counselor must be careful not to be seduced by the counselee's pain to the extent that counseling objectives and the ability to provide wise counsel are lost.

The pastoral counselor can help with spiritual and relational issues and must be diligent to keep counseling goals and priorities straight. It is advised that the pastoral counselor only counsel people with mild disorders who are partnering with their physician and taking their medications as prescribed. Many who have the diagnosis of mental illness do not like the side effects of medication and take less medication than their doctor has prescribed or stop taking them it all together. These common practices will have adverse effects on the patient. Be sure to inquire about compliance with doctor's orders.

Some may come for counseling without disclosing that they have been previously diagnosed with a mood disorder or mental illness. They may not immediately reveal that they have been prescribed medications, or that they are currently not taking them as prescribed, or at all. If the counselee refuses to take medication as prescribed by their doctor it is recommended that the counselor make taking medication as prescribed a condition for counseling or terminate the counseling relationship.

Typically, the pastoral counselor is not a medical health professional. When they are, they know it is malpractice to offer an opinion to someone who is not their patient. The pastoral counselor has no opinion about the medication a doctor has prescribed for the counselee.

Even when the counselor has had personal experience with a medication they must reserve their opinion and suggest the counselee consult their doctor before making any changes to their medical regimen. The counselor's role is to encourage the counselee to partner with their physician and take medication as prescribed.

Thought and emotional problems are often brought to pastoral counselors. Many individuals come for counsel when they are experiencing the negative consequences of thought and emotional problems. A thought or emotional problem manifests in a pattern of faulty thinking that has led to actions resulting in personal, relation, or spiritual dysfunction.

A thought or emotional problem is not necessarily a mood disorder or mental illness. It may be a result of a lifetime of habitual behavior and relational patterns that have never been interrupted by faith, reason, or necessity. In some cases, an ultimatum has been given to the counselee regarding their irrational behavior resulting from faulty thoughts and emotions that have negatively impacted their relationships. It is often as a last resort that the individual is willing to consider the possibility of change.

Paranoia can be an extreme pattern of unhealthy thought where the predominant feature is distrust of others. A person who is paranoid is often unwilling to forgive others. Paranoia can present as a heightened level of suspicion of others. When paranoia is connected with mood disorders or mental illness, a person may be suspicious of everyone. Paranoia isolated from mood disorders and mental illness is often more focused on people the counselee believes can cause them emotional pain.

In an emotional or thought problem, paranoia and facts are often incompatible.

Providing care and insight for the person who mistrusts everyone presents challenges to the counselor best met with patience and persistence. Allow time for a relationship of trust to build, remembering the counselee is most likely suspicious of you. Understand that they will be guarded and secretive regarding information about themselves. Encourage the counselee to keep track of their thoughts throughout the day, noticing their thinking patterns.

Help individuals who have been harmed by the behaviors of someone expressing paranoid thoughts to find their voice and speak out against negative and irrational behaviors. Help the wounded person see the incompatibility between unhealthy thought and emotional patterns and the reality of their circumstances.

Often, the individual causing harm lives primarily in isolation from community interaction that might hold them accountable. They have been permitted to live out unhealthy and harmful patterns of relating that have caused damage to their relationships. Suggest they get connected or reconnected with a support system.

When it comes to mental disorders and thought and emotional problems it is imperative that the counselor offer "The Rule of Hope." The "Rule of Hope" demonstrates the counselor's belief they can help the counselee by making a difference in the quality of their spiritual, relational, and emotional life.

Bringing the counselee into right relationship with Christ is primary to building an understanding of how best to conduct relationships with others. Loving from a biblical perspective has the ability to transform thinking and behavior, equipping the counselee to experience joy, peace, hope, and healing. When the counselee is able to discover and claim God's promises he or she will truly experience the abundant life every believer is promised.

The thief comes only to steal and kill and destroy; I came that they might have life, and have it abundantly.
John 10:10

When the counselee is motivated by their love for God and empowered by the presence of the Holy Spirit there is certainty of true hope and joy.

"Hope is informed optimism." — Michael J. Fox[44]

Left to patterns of unhealthy thinking, influenced by the enemy, individuals will be robbed of their rightful inheritance as children of the living God. With information and encouragement, the counselee can experience the best quality of life.

Let us hold fast the confession of our hope without
wavering, for He who promised is faithful; and let us
consider how to stimulate one another to love and good
deeds. Hebrews 10:23, 24

Suicide

Suicide has become more common in today's culture. It remains, however, a permanent solution to a temporary problem.

"Every 14 minutes someone dies by suicide.
Every 15 minutes someone else is left trying to make sense of it."
—American Foundation for Suicide Prevention

Often there is a conspiracy of silence around the topic of suicide. Many suffer in silence and secrecy, unwilling to discuss their painful thoughts. This serious reality is a topic that must be addressed. Bringing the subject of suicide into the light has the potential to prevent someone from making this devastating choice.

Suicide impacts a broad spectrum of the population. The Center for Disease Control and Prevention reported on suicides in the U.S. by age group in 2013. The CDC reports that suicide is the second leading cause of death for people aged

25–34; the third leading cause of death for people aged 10–24; and, the fourth leading cause of death for adults between the ages of 18 and 65.[45]

The profile of someone considering suicide is often described as a person who feels overwhelmed and is not thinking clearly. Often, these people really don't want to die. They are hurting and believe the only way to stop the pain is to go away.

There are indications of suicidal tendencies that can be recognized and must be addressed. One of the most effective tools to prevent suicide is to ask questions. Often the suicidal person has allowed their thoughts of suicide to dominate their thinking to the point they seem commonplace. All talk of suicide must be taken seriously. To help prevent and minimize the risk of suicide there must be a basic understanding of the dynamics of suicidal talk.

You don't have to be a mind reader when it comes to suicide. The key is to listen and respond to any and all suicidal talk. There are two types of suicidal talk. The first is active suicide talk.

Active suicide talk is simple and straightforward. You don't have to guess what's going on. Active suicide talk may sound something like this:

- "I just want to put the gun to my head and put an end to all this pain."
- "I feel like getting in my car and driving as fast as I can into a cement pole."

- "I have a bunch of pills at home and I know that it would put me to sleep."
- "I'm so tired and just want to die."

The second type of suicide talk is passive suicide talk. This type of talk is an indirect style of speech. Passive suicide talk can sometimes not be recognized because it's so subtle. It may sound something like this:

- "I was thinking the family would be better off if I wasn't around."
- "I'm worth a lot more dead than I am alive."
- "I want to go to sleep and never wake up."
- "I'm not sure I can take much more of this pain."

Another concern when addressing the risk of suicide is suicidal thought. Often thoughts of suicide have been present in a person's thoughts for a period of time before they manifest in speech. Thoughts of suicide are a serious concern. Frequent thoughts of suicide are defined as daily, weekly, or monthly. Any thought of suicide is a thought too many. To detect patterns of suicidal thought in the counselee, the counselor must be aware of the counselee's thought patterns. The counselor must ask probing questions that reveal information about suicidal thought. The pastoral counselor must help the individual recognize the seriousness of their unhealthy thought life, create an awareness of the negative thought patterns and help the individual address them. To ignore unhealthy patterns of suicidal thought or talk would be no different than to ignore a serious wound as it festered to the point of becoming life threatening.

Thought life can seriously impair judgment, shape unhealthy attitudes, and inform poor choices. There must be conscious and intentional effort to take every thought captive to the obedience of Christ.

We use our powerful God-tools for smashing warped philosophies, tearing down barriers erected against the truth of God, fitting every loose thought and emotion and impulse into the structure of life shaped by Christ.
2 Corinthians 10:5 (MSG)

Passive suicidal thought allows the person to daydream about dying to the point they become comfortable with the idea of dying or simply not being around. When an individual has fanaticized about not being around, they see the idea of suicide as a positive solution to their painful dilemma. Suicidal thought has started to become a reality in this person's mind. Suicidal thought has taken shape in a way that has become an acceptable option or solution.

When assessing the risk of suicide there are several important questions to ask. Ask if suicide has been attempted in the past. When an individual has attempted suicide in the past they typically learned something. This knowledge can prove deadly should they make a second attempt. The man or woman who has gone online to discover the ingredients for a cocktail that might end their life discovers when he or she wakes up the next morning that the attempt has failed. Armed with new knowledge, they may try again, this time succeeding.

The pastoral counselor must be bold and diligent in the pursuit of answers to questions about suicide. Ask if there is a plan to act on the threat of suicide. Ask if the plan is lethal, and if there is a way to implement it. Ask questions to discover if the counselee is experiencing a sense of hopelessness. Ask is they are relationally or socially isolated. Ask if they are bringing closure to their affairs.

Suicide is the ultimate act of futility sending a message that there was no other option, or better way to address the pain in the individual's life. Suicide declares that the individual has given up, taken the easy way out, failed to rely on the help of God and others, or avail themselves to resources designed to remedy the situation. The person considering suicide often lacks the courage and tenacity to find the way to make the best of their circumstances, allowing these circumstances to destroy rather than develop them. They allowed their pain to define them, rather than their identity in Christ. The counselor must do everything they can within reason to prevent this horrific choice from becoming a permanent solution to a temporary problem.

The counselor must remind the person talking of suicide that it is one of the meanest things they can do to those who are left behind. Those who are left behind wonder what they should have, could have, or might have done to prevent this. A parent who takes their own life sends the unhealthy message to their children that suicide is a viable option when life gets tough. Suicide is a deadly message to give children.

In a study led by Johns Hopkins Children's Center it is reported that losing a parent to suicide makes children more likely to die by suicide and increases their risk of developing a range of major psychiatric disorders. When children or teens lose a parent to suicide they are three times more likely to commit suicide.[46]

If the counselee asks if they will go to Hell if they commit suicide, be prepared to give a carefully considered answer. We know what the Bible says when a person professes their belief in Jesus Christ they receive the gift of eternal life. The Fifth Commandment, "Thou shalt not kill," applies to taking one's own life. While this is a serious sin it is not unforgivable and will not take away salvation. Suicide is not the unpardonable sin. Ask first what the counselee believes. Never contradict Scripture, but if possible allow the counselee to have some doubt. This just might impact their decision.

After assessing the risk of suicide for the counselee take appropriate action. Insist the counselee take the steps listed below. If the counselee resists or refuses it is imperative that the proper authorities be called so the individual can be held in a manner that will secure their safety. Confidentiality is waived when the threat of suicide is imminent.

When the risk of suicide is high, have the counselee call their doctor immediately. If getting an appointment the same day isn't possible, ensure that the counselee gets to a local emergency room to be evaluated and receive treatment until their primary care doctor can be seen.

Have the counselee contact someone to stay with them for the next few days. Staying with a loved one or having someone stay with the individual is key in this stage of prevention.

If the individual indicated they plan to use pills or a gun, have them allow a friend or family member remove the pills or gun from the home. Should it be necessary, contact the proper authorities to remove a weapon from the counselee's home, car, or office.

Have the counselee sign an agreement with you that they will not attempt to hurt themselves until they see you first. Do not give the counselee your personal phone number or address. Instead, insist they agree to *see* you, not *call* you, before an attempt is made to harm themselves.

Suicide is a permanent solution to a temporary problem. All thought and talk of suicide must be taken seriously and addressed immediately. The stakes are too high to ignore the problem.

Trauma

Trauma is defined as a bodily injury, shock or wound, or a psychological injury that can produce lasting effects.[47]

Sometimes trauma is both bodily and psychological injury. Trauma is something unexpected. Rarely is the individual prepared for it. Trauma can ambush, like a deviant enemy with evil intentions masquerading as a friend, colleague, or family member.

A traumatic event can "…shatter the sense of connection between individual and community, creating a crisis of faith."[48]

Trauma often leaves the individual in a state of despair. "Trauma means living with the recurrent, tormenting memories of atrocities witnessed or borne. Memories that infect victims' sleep with horrific nightmares destroy their relationships or their capacity to work or study, torment their emotions, shatter their faith and mutilate hope."[49]

The pastoral counselor must teach a person wounded by trauma not to trust what appears to be the certainties of despair. "Despair is relentless in the certainties of its pessimism. But we have seen again and again, from our own experience and others, the absolute statements of hopelessness that we make in the dark are notoriously unreliable."[50]

The pastoral counselor must encourage the victim of trauma to discover God's faithfulness to heal and his desire to show compassion.

Trauma impacts the individual spiritually, emotionally, psychologically and physically. Manifestations of spiritual impact can include hopelessness, loss of purpose, self-doubt, or a crisis of faith. The emotional effects of trauma can include powerlessness, anxiety, anger, or mistrust. The psychological effects of trauma can manifest in fear, confusion, obsession with trauma, negative thought, or denial. The physical effects of trauma can include sleep disturbances, addictions, impaired immune system, and harmful or risky behaviors.

To mitigate the effects of trauma the counselor must help the counselee take steps toward healing and hope. The journey to the wholeness begins with honesty before God, self, and others. Telling the truth about what has happened is often very frightening. Living in denial is sometimes much easier. Distractions of lesser pursuit such as busyness, obsessions, addictions, or harmful behaviors can keep the individual from healing. It's important to help the counselee look honestly at where they are in the healing process. Maybe they haven't even begun the journey. Often the individual will deceive him- or herself, making up stories to tell that cover the truth. Lies become truth. Negative self-talk becomes a weapon of self-destruction. The individual becomes his or her own worst enemy.

The heart is more deceitful than all else and is desperately sick; who can understand it? Jeremiah 17:9

The world is broken. Sin wreaks havoc with God's plans. God gave man free will. Unfortunately, this permits others to do harm. Help the counselee see that this is their time to begin the healing process and see it through. It is their time to laugh, their time to dance and enjoy the good plans God has for them, in spite of what has happened. Help the counselee see that it is no coincidence they are in counseling now. Help them see that there is a time for everything.

A time to weep and a time to laugh; a time to mourn and a time to dance. Ecclesiastes 3:4

Help the counselee see it is time to begin the journey to wholeness and health—a journey that begins with one step. Ask if they are willing to take that first step. Encourage them that together you can discover the good plans God has for them.

"For I know the plans that I have for you," declares the Lord, "plans for welfare and not for calamity to give you a future and a hope." Jeremiah 29:11

Ask the counselee if they are up for the challenge and willing to hear God's voice and respond. This can be a scary thought for the counselee. They may be in disbelief, thinking this is all too good to be true. Maybe they don't believe any of it at all. Maybe they don't even believe in God at this time in their journey. Tell them that it is okay...God believes in them.

He has numbered the hairs on their head, knows everything about them, and still loves them unconditionally. Help the individual come to see that God's greatest desire is to be close to them. It is why they were created.

Help the individual become the person God designed them to be and receive his blessing of healing and hope.

For we are God's masterpiece. He has created us anew in Christ Jesus, so we can do the good things he planned for us long ago. Ephesians 2:10 (NLT)

Help them see that they were created for the abundant life. They are God's masterpiece and worthy of healing and restored hope.

Do not fear, for I have redeemed you; I have called you by name; you are Mine! Isaiah 43:1

Why is God so good to us? Why does he continue to show grace and mercy when it is undeserved?

In his book *The Furious Longing of God*, Brennan Manning writes about God's crazy love. Searching for words to describe the startling reality of God's love, he writes:

"...the shattering truth of the transcendent God seeking intimacy with us is not well served by gauzy sentimentality, schmaltz, or a naked appeal to emotion, but rather in the boiling bouillabaisse of shock bordering on disbelief, wonder akin to incredulity, and affectionate awe tinged by doubt."[51]

Shock and wonder can be the experience of God's love. Remarkably abundant, shamelessly undeserved...often overlooked. For the unbeliever, God's love becomes a sad reality of missed opportunity. Seize the moment to share his love with the counselee who is hurting, confused, and feeling hopeless.

Pray for the counselee that they will come to know God's love for them with "wonder akin to incredulity, and affectionate awe tinged by doubt." Pray that in the reality of God's love they will find the joy and contentment Jesus planned. Pray they will embrace God's mercies, which are new every morning, with the wide-eyed enthusiasm of a child.

Grief and Loss

When a loved one dies or the diagnosis is cancer it is easy to withdraw from life feeling lost and alone. Loss can define, destroy, or develop individuals. Loss can debilitate to the point of hopelessness. In grief and loss there are choices to make. It will take effort, intentionality, and God's help to develop character and build identity in Christ to face loss or tragedy.

Grieving is a process. It is different for everyone. There is no right way or specific length of time to grieve. Elisabeth Kübler-Ross describes the five stages of grief as: denial, anger, bargaining, depression, and acceptance.[52] Some may move back and forth between the stages. Helping the counselee discover which stage they are in is a first step in grief counseling. There are excellent grief programs available in most communities like Grief Share, (www.griefshare.org), designed to help people who have suffered recent loss. Encourage the counselee to attend. Participation in grief counseling curriculum with those who have suffered loss can be helpful to many. Walking with the counselee as they participate in a grief counseling program can also be beneficial. The pastoral counselor can help the counselee avoid some pitfalls in the process.

The counselee may be someone who has never healed from a loss or trauma that occurred many years earlier. Still, encourage participation in a grief program and walk with the counselee to help them move forward in the healing process.

While some move back and forth between the stages, others may become stuck in one stage or another. As individuals go through the grieving process they must be encouraged to avoid the temptation to deny their humanity. They must give themselves permission to grieve.

Jesus did.

John writes in Chapter 11, verse 35 that when Lazarus died, "Jesus wept." Sometimes the counselee may be up on a down day, other times they may not. It's ok. It will get better, maybe just not today.

Expectations play a role in the grieving process. Ask the counselee who they expect to comfort them in their time of loss. The person they most want comfort from may not be able to give it. Friends and family sometimes have an inability to bear grief, or a fear of saying or doing the wrong thing, so they back away, just when they are needed most. Decades can pass, leaving grief unresolved, taking its toll on relationships and robbing the bereft of joy.

Another potentially harmful expectation is the unrealistic expectation of others that the person grieving should be better by now, able to get over it, and no longer feel sad. Grief often makes others uncomfortable.

Healing from loss is a process, one that begins with an awareness of God's unfailing love, of his power and faithfulness to intervene on the grief-stricken person's behalf. The counselor's role is to help the counselee see the Lord's plan and purpose in suffering, never asking "why," always asking "what." Encourage the counselee to ask the right question to help them discover what can be learned from this experience and how it can be used to encourage others.

Loss takes many forms. It might be the child who strayed from God's path who doesn't return as expected, the spouse who abandoned the marriage who doesn't come home, or the loved one with cancer who doesn't get healed. Help the counselee fix their eyes on Jesus rather than the pain. It might seem an unrealistic request in the moment, or in the face of such an unspeakable event. The counselor will need to be sensitive to the timing of the loss, allowing the counselee time to process raw and painful emotions, especially in the initial stages of loss.

A different approach is taken when the individual has had a significant amount of time, perhaps decades, to process their grief. They may be stuck, unable to move from shock and denial to acceptance, failing to resolve their grief. When the individual's identity is defined by loss or tragedy, rather than relationship with Christ, it can become a "mistaken identity" limiting the individual's potential for joy, hope, and healing.

Observe the counselee's conversations. Are they more about the loss and difficulties they have experienced than the redeeming love of God and the resulting contentment it brings? When the counselee is stuck, stalled out in the quagmire of their story, however horrific it might be, help them see that God wants to change their perspective. Help them see that God can and will redeem their story if they will let him. Show them the way to transform their identity from loss to a legacy of love defined by their identity in Christ.

"Though no one can go back and make a brand-new start, my friend, anyone can start from now and make a brand-new ending." —Carl Bard

---

God has written and played the key role in the story of salvation, which promises to redeem our stories, mending what it broken, healing what is sick, making right what has gone wrong. The story of redemption promises to envelop and transform all other stories, however sensational or mundane, tragic or happy.

"God redeems our stories through his. If you dare to surrender yourself to God, he will take up the story of your life and integrate it into the great story of salvation, turning it into something so extraordinary that you will be tempted to think that it was all a beautiful dream."[53]

We lose to gain, die to live, and renounce to inherit. True freedom is found in surrender that comes from knowing, trusting, and obeying God. It is the counselor's role to walk beside their counselee as they discover God's redemptive plan for their story.

God calls for triumph through suffering, to accomplish a vision, great or small, for his kingdom. God calls for transformation from brokenness to blessing.

In the healing process, there are four steps that can be taken that will help move the counselee in the right direction. Moving from loss to a legacy of love can be accomplished through these four steps. Encourage the counselee to be intentional in this process.

First, **believe** in him and trust his faithfulness. Second, **behold** the wonder of his greatness and discover depth and breadth of his character. Third, **become** the person God intends, allowing the knowledge of his Word to inform choices, attitudes, and behaviors. And fourth **bless** the next generation with a legacy of love expressed in joy and contentment that encourages others and brings glory and honor to God.

Step one — In step one, encourage the individual to fix their eyes on Jesus and learn to believe in him and trust his faithfulness. Help them see that staying stuck in the past keeps a legacy of love from unfolding. With a better understanding of who Jesus is and how to believe what he says, the counselee can gain the understanding that hanging on to past hurts mocks God.

Therefore the Lord longs to be gracious to you, and therefore He waits on high to have compassion on you.
Isaiah 30:18

Help the counselee learn how to receive God's loving-kindness, remember his faithfulness and claim his promises. Ask if God has brought them through tough times before. Help them list those occurrences and reflect on the outcome. Remind them they can trust his provision and that he will meet their needs.

And my God will supply all your needs according to His riches in glory in Christ Jesus. Philippians 4:19

Step two — In step two help the counselee behold the wonder of God's greatness.

The limited human mind cannot grasp the vastness and complexity of God's creation. Recent findings confirm that the perimeters of the universe have yet to be defined. New galaxies continue to be discovered declaring the wonders of God's infinite ability.

The heavens are telling of the glory of God; and their expanse is declaring the work of His hands. Psalm 19:1

Knowing God's Word helps in the discovery of the depth and breadth of his character. The Old Testament is full of stories of God's loving-kindness toward his people. Time and again man failed to keep the covenants God made with him, yet God continued to demonstrate his desire to draw him into relationship through the renewal of covenantal agreements. God still seeks to restore broken people through his abundant loving-kindness and faithfulness. His compassions never fail.

Because of the Lord's great love we are not consumed, for his compassions never fail. They are new every morning; great is your faithfulness. Lamentations 3:22, 23 (NIV)

To behold God's character, one must seek him with all their heart, mind, and soul. The promise from Scripture is that when we do this we will find him.

You will seek Me and find Me when you search for Me
with all your heart. Jeremiah 29:13

In **step three** — help the counselee become a new creation.

Therefore if anyone is in Christ, he is a new creature; the
old things passed away; behold, new things have come.
2 Corinthians 5:17

The promise that anyone who is "in Christ" is a new creature is both a privilege and a responsibility. It's a miraculous
privilege that God can transform a life from trauma to healing,
from tragedy to triumph and from despair to hope. It is each
individual's responsibility to do all he or she can to make this
happen. It will take conscious effort to believe that old things
have passed away and new things have come. Breaking free
from the bondage of past hurts frees the individual to experience God's best. It is the counselor's role to instruct and
encourage them along the way.

Living in denial won't allow the process to begin. Living
distracted by busyness won't allow the time. Destructive
behaviors like addictions, self-mutilation, or negative self-talk
will not facilitate the healing process. Help the counselee see if
they are practicing unhealthy behaviors that are keeping them
from healing. Encourage them to learn and adopt new spiritual
disciplines and healthy habits to facilitate growth and healing.

Help the counselee discover ways to be transformed by taking every thought captive.

And do not be conformed to this world, but be transformed by the renewing of your mind, so that you may prove what the will of God is, that which is good and acceptable and perfect. Romans 12:2

There may be strongholds in the counselee's life keeping them from taking the first step and becoming who God has designed them to be. Strongholds of shame, guilt, or unforgiveness can keep a person in bondage, unable and unwilling to participate in the healing process.

Shame is an inner torment that attacks a person's very worth. Shame strikes deep in the heart, offering an incorrect definition of who the individual is. Encouraging the counselee to be identified by their relationship with Christ will help keep shame from undermining God's grace and purpose.

Guilt can also shackle a person keeping them in bondage to past sin. Help the counselee fully embrace God's forgiveness.

As far as the east is from the west, so far has He removed our transgressions from us. Psalm 103:12

Unforgiveness can keep a person in bondage. Encourage the counselee to trust God to know what is best. Help the counselee understand both the biblical definition and the healing power of forgiveness. It is a difficult process to be forgiving and forgiven people; it takes time and involves struggle.

In order to become all that God intends, individuals must be intentional in their prayer life. Encourage the adoption of the practice of spiritual disciplines. The practice of good spiritual disciplines takes the individual beyond surface living into the depths, urging him or her to dwell deep in a shallow world. Teach the counselee the importance of practicing the inward spiritual disciplines of meditation, prayer, fasting, and study; the outward spiritual disciplines of simplicity, solitude, submission, and service; and, the corporate disciplines of confession, worship, guidance, and celebration.[54] (A further discussion on the practice of spiritual disciplines is found in Chapter Five.)

Becoming a man or woman of Christ involves surrender.

"You must come to be utterly helpless, to let God work, and God will work gloriously."[55]

As the individual surrenders their hurts, habits, and hang-ups they will move forward in the healing process. It's risky business to rely only on one's individual strength and ability. The mistake often made is to go as far as one can on his or her own strength, and *then* ask God for help. The winning formula is to come *first* to God, asking him to supply what is needed.

And my God will supply all your needs according to His riches in glory in Christ Jesus. Philippians 4:19

It's a difficult challenge to set aside pride and self-perceived invincibility and ask for help. Recognizing our helplessness, we must worship the omnipotent God who will work in us every moment. This is God's truth. This is the truth that sets us free! Firmly grounded in the promises of God, we are equipped to do what is required in the healing process. It might look impossible, but we are promised possible.

Jesus said, "The things that are impossible with people are possible with God." Luke 18:27

Pray the Lord will lead the counselee out of the spirit of bondage into the spirit of liberty, from self-reliance to complete dependence on God that he or she may find hope again. Remind them that when they are feeling insufficient to the task, God is not. Weakness is perfected in his power.

My grace is sufficient for you, for power is perfected in weakness. 2 Corinthians 12:9a

Step four — is about leaving a legacy of love that will bless the next generation. The final step in the process of moving from loss to legacy is to share with others the testimony of God's faithfulness. Sharing God's faithfulness includes boasting in his power and provision.

Most gladly, therefore, I will rather boast about my
weaknesses, so that the power of Christ may dwell in me.
2 Corinthians 12:9b

As individuals live out this final step they must be mindful of their communication, asking what messages they are giving to friends, family, and others. What legacy are they leaving? Is the counselee leaving a message of hope, healing, and God's power, or a legacy of loss, despair, and hopelessness? Have they allowed their loss to define, develop, or destroy them? Ask the counselee what they would like their legacy to be. Ask how they want to be remembered. Have them write a paragraph describing what might be said if they transformed their loss into a legacy of love.

A legacy of love is demonstrated in the person who trusts God's plan and purpose for their life. A legacy of love is expressed in love rather than loss, bearing witness to the hope there is in a relationship with Christ. This life bears witness to the reality that in Christ all things are possible.

Often the key to grieving a loss or healing from trauma lies in the counselee's ability to find purpose and community.

Followers of Christ are meant to be a part of the community of faith. Believing in Christ includes belonging to his family. In God's family believers pursue their passion and find purpose.

Help the counselee discover what opportunities best match their skills, heart, aptitude, passion and experience in this season of life. Weekly attendance at a worship service, involvement in a small group Bible study, and participation in ministry are but a few of the ways the counselee can connect with others. Isolation is detrimental to moving forward in the healing process or finding hope. Helping the counselee discover, or rediscover, their purpose has a significant impact on their healing from loss or trauma.

Help the counselee explore the possibilities for connection available to them in the community where they live or work. Avoid being the counselee's only source of social interaction. You are not the counselee's friend, you are their counselor. Setting the counselee up for success includes maintaining healthy boundaries. From this perspective you are better able to see the ideal solution. Help the counselee find ways to discover and pursue their passion and to connect or reconnect with friends, family, and community. Serving in ministry is always a good way to find both purpose and community. Have the counselee make the discoveries, stopping short of doing for them what they need to do for themselves.

Sharing Your Testimony

Be ready to give a reason for the hope you have.

*Sanctify Christ as Lord in your hearts, always being
ready to make a defense to everyone who asks you to give
an account for the hope that is in you.* 1 Peter 3:15

The counseling process is not about the counselor. There will be times, however, when telling some of your testimony will help the counseling process. It may be with few or many details. Let the Holy Spirit guide you to the right amount of sharing. You may talk briefly about surviving a divorce, the loss of a child, or cancer, telling just enough of the story to give your witness credibility and encourage the counselee that they too can survive their trial, tragedy, or trauma.

The counselor must exercise discretion so as not to distract the counselee with their personal pain. Stop short of sharing all of the details of an egregious event or traumatic loss in your life as this may take the counseling session in the wrong direction. The counselee may become so distracted by the counselor's pain or challenge they feel better focusing on you rather than on their own issues. This practice can be counterproductive to the counseling process.

The counselor must also be careful not to establish him- or herself as the standard for successful counseling. When the counselor appears to have done everything right, the counselee falls into the trap of comparison, thinking that next to the counselor, they fall short. This may discourage the counselee and worse, the counselee may begin to factor God's plan out of the equation and miss the path he is directing them to follow.

The counselor must be careful to maintain a close connection to God, covering every session in prayer, practicing good spiritual disciplines and hearing God's voice to know when the time is right and how much to share from their personal testimony.

Let your light shine before men in such a way that they may see your good works, and glorify your Father who is in heaven. Matthew 5:16

Questions for Consideration

1. List three ways you would help a couple see that their marriage is more about honoring God than meeting their needs.
2. What principles are common to parenting in a biological family and a blended family?
3. When it comes to mental illness, name three things the pastoral counselor must remember.
4. Briefly describe the two types of suicide talk.
5. What is one of the most important things to do when a counselee is talking about suicide?

CHAPTER FOUR

Getting Started in the Counseling Process

Get to Know the Counselee

It takes time to build a relationship of trust with a counselee. Go slow in developing a foundation for successful counseling, demonstrating care about the little things as well as the big things. Take notes in the initial sessions to remember important data about the counselee's life and relationships.

Ask the counselee(s) what they hope to gain in the counseling experience. Ask about their desired outcome from counseling. Help the counselee clearly articulate the reason they have come for counseling.

Ask probing questions to discover the counselee's story. Where were they born? Where were they raised? Do they have siblings? Did they grow up in a two-parent home? What was and is their relationship with their parents and siblings? Have them tell you about their education, work experience, and relationship history. This time of discovery may take several sessions. The time invested early in the relationship will yield dividends in the future.

Gaining a better understanding of the counselee's relational history will be indicative of their willingness to work toward resolving their issues. Notice patterns of reasonableness versus rigidness. Is the counselee one to take the steps necessary to resolve problems? Or are they inflexible or unwilling to take the risks necessary to either solve problems or establish new patterns of behavior? Is the counselee one who blames others for their failures in relationship or are they willing to take responsibility, even when they are only a small part of the problem? What did the counselee learn about conflict management skills growing up? Did they have parents who were emotionally unavailable, substance abusive, or violent?

Each of these factors will contribute to how the counselee conducts their current relationships. Help the counselee recognize any unhealthy patterns of behavior and teach new skills that will set them up for success in their relationships. Help them focus on the positive rather than the negative aspects of their relationships.

Finally, brethren, whatever is true, whatever is honorable,
whatever is right, whatever is pure, whatever is lovely,
whatever is of good repute, if there is any excellence
and if anything worthy of praise, dwell on these things.
Philippians 4:8

Inquire about the counselee's relationship with God. Do they have a personal relationship with Jesus? Ask about their spiritual habits.

Have the counselee tell you about their relationship with God and its current condition. Ask if their relationship with God has ever been different than it is now. Ask if they have every committed their life to Christ.

Knowing where the counselee stands in their walk with the Lord is critical to how you provide counsel. Making these discoveries early in the counseling process informs the pastoral counselor as to the direction for their counsel, toward discipleship or evangelism. This phase of information gathering will help craft a dialogue that is appropriate for the individual. Be careful not to speak "Christianese" to a non-believer as this may not be encouraging and might even send them out the door. Be careful not to make assumptions when a counselee professes faith in Jesus. Inquire about their spiritual habits, church attendance, and Bible reading. Make informed observations that will equip you with the right words, tone, and demeanor for the individual. Be self-aware as you speak to the counselee, making every effort to be respectful yet direct, affirming but never judging. Express your faith in patience, kindness, and gentleness.

But the fruit of the Spirit is love, joy, peace, patience, kindness, goodness faithfulness, gentleness, self-control; against such things there is no law. Galatians 5:22

As you observe the counselee, assess their personality type, thinking style, and love language. There are many good resources available to help the counselee discover who they are and how they prefer to express themselves in relationship to others.

The Meyers & Briggs Personality test is a good indicator of how the counselee is wired.[56] Knowing if one is an extrovert or introvert will help determine the best way to renew energy and refresh the spirit. The introvert will typically recharge in solitude whereas the extrovert prefers the company of others. Knowing if one is sensing, judging, or intuitive reveals how information is processed and decisions are made.

Learning the counselee's love language is helpful in determining what they want in relationship. Does the counselee prefer words of affirmation, quality time, gifts, acts of service, or physical touch?[57] Encourage the counselee to know their love language and the love language of those they are in relationship with.

Take time to observe the counselee's thinking style. Discovering the thinking style of the counselee helps the counselor understand how the individual may have arrived at the conclusions that have brought them in for counseling.

Is the counselee's thinking style fragmented or enmeshed? The fragmented thinker doesn't typically see the connection between events, whereas the enmeshed thinker often connects events in an exaggerated manner. The fragmented thinker is quick to forgive, while the enmeshed thinker keeps a record of wrongs sometimes spanning decades.

Does the counselee demonstrate a thinking style that reveals they are a thinker or a feeler? Do they arrange their thoughts in an orderly fashion and analyze them before making decisions? Or are they a feeler, more likely to relate to and understand experience through emotional reactions and responses to their feelings? Is their thinking style that of a sensor, someone whose experiences are based mainly on personal sensory perceptions or "gut feelings?" Or are they one whose thinking style is intuitive, given to projection of intention based on what they perceive or induce in the situation?

Teaching the fragmented thinker to see the connection between events may help them learn the impact of failing to keep agreements. Helping the enmeshed thinker let go of events from the past may help them learn to forgive loved ones they have been holding hostage for decades. Helping the person who is a thinker recognize that they sometimes overthink things may help them recognize what's brought them to the point of inactivity or what might appear to be apathy. Helping the sensor see that always responding to their "gut feelings" may lead them to misperception of an event or communication may open them to resolving hurt feelings. The intuitive thinker may need to learn that sometimes their perception of reality is false, causing them to project incorrect or inappropriate emotions in to a situation.

No one personality type, love language or thinking style is superior to another. Observing the differences in the counselee helps the counselor recognize unhealthy or destructive patterns of thinking and relating. Teaching the counselee new ways of thinking and behaving based in biblical authority helps to improve the counselee's relationships.

What is the counselee's "theology of conflict?" This discovery is key to helping the counselee resolve conflict. Help the counselee develop healthy conflict management skills, based in common sense and informed by Christian values. After reviewing the information presented in Chapter Two on Conflict Management, inquire as to the type of conflict management style the counselee has. Does the counselee see conflict as a natural, neutral, and inevitable part of relationship? Are they willing to be collaborative in resolving conflict, or do they avoid conflict at any cost? Is the counselee more inclined to be combative when it comes to conflict resolution, choosing to confront the matter in an angry or aggressive manner? Help the counselee discover their conflict management style and learn that in life affirming, God-honoring conflict management behaviors align with biblical principles and direct the course of resolution.

Teach those who are avoidant to find their voice and engage in conversations to resolve conflict. Help the aggressive or combative individual recognize their dominant style and make necessary adjustments. Set the counselee up to win in conversations about conflict. When engaging in conversations about conflict management encourage the participants to adhere to the following guidelines:

- Establish a time suitable to both parties.
- Determine a location that is private, quiet, and neutral.
- Open the discussion with prayer.
- Be mindful of body language, being careful to be open and relaxed.
- Use "I" statements to describe thoughts, feelings, or desires.
- Define the issue to be discussed.
- Avoid using profanity.
- Do not interrupt.
- Find resolution agreeable to both parties.
- Close in prayer.

Help the counselee discover that conflict resolved from a Christian perspective provides redemptive, win/win options. Teach the counselee to be aware of their personal theology of conflict and make adjustments that will honor God and improve their relationships with others.

Inquire about the counselee's identity in Christ. When asked to define him- or herself, does the counselee respond by describing their roles, relationships, achievements or the opinions of others? If so, this reveals their identity is not in Christ. The roles every individual has change throughout life. People grow from children to adolescents and then to adults. Daughters and sons see their roles change with time, as do parents. Some define themselves by their achievements or career, such as being a teacher, doctor, or lawyer. Maybe they define themselves as being an athlete or beauty queen.

Some define themselves by the opinions of others. When individuals seek significance in roles that are temporary they experience mistaken identity that will not sustain their sense of self for a lifetime. Only one role is permanent in a person's life. This role is defined in relationship with Christ and is that of being a child of God. In relationship with Christ, every individual is a new creation—the old has passed, new things have come.

In Christ, everyone has the capability to be who he or she was designed by God to be. Even when the individual falls short of accomplishing great things or meeting the expectations of others, they are whole, complete, and unconditionally loved by God. Introducing the counselee to this reality can transform their thinking and help them experience the joy, hope, and healing God has planned for them. Teaching the counselee the reality of God's unconditional love for them can set them free to enjoy the abundant life God planned for them. Learning that in relationship with the living God there is nothing to prove, individuals can experience that they are whole, complete, and loved by the creator of the universe. When this truth sets them free they have the ability to forgive and move forward. They can develop the ability to accept and love significant others who may have never offered the unconditional love, acceptance, or affirmation the counselee so desperately sought. From this position they can discover, refine, and use their gifts and talents, offering them back to God in acts of worship.

I can do all things through Him who strengthens me.
Philippians 4:13

Define the Presenting Problem

Ask probing questions that will help define the presenting problem. Start with very general, non-threatening questions. Go slow and build a relationship of trust. Demonstrate interest in the little things in the counselee's life that create the foundation for the expression of the bigger things.

If the counselee makes a broad statement about what they see as the main problem, such as "I feel sad," help them find more descriptive words and illustrations so that the true nature of the problem can be clearly defined. Often what the counselee thinks is the presenting problem is not.

As you help them refine what they see as the problem, it may shift a few times before settling on the true problem. It is critical that the counselor avoids generalities and is specific when defining the presenting problem.

Establish Counseling Goal

Once the presenting problem has been clearly articulated, establish counseling goals. It is important to be specific when establishing goals. If the counseling goal is to improve communication with a spouse, be clear about what type of communication the counselee means. A clearer goal would be to "improve communication about consistent discipline regarding the children," defining the area of communication the counselee wishes to see improvement in.

Next, together with the counselee define what the results will look like when the counseling goal is met. Be specific and define a result that is measurable. For instance, "have a daily, ten-minute conversation about discipline." The more detailed the definition of the result is, the better chance the counselee has to see results. Vague and indifferent responses to this question will net ineffective and unsustainable results. Always set the counselee up to win by establishing clear, measurable results.

As the presenting problem is defined, it may become clear that there is more than one goal the counselee wants to address. Have them agree to work on one goal at a time. Once a counseling goal has been met it is time to talk about working on a new goal. Keeping the counselee focused on one goal at a time allows for the focus and energy necessary to incorporate changes that are transformative and sustainable.

Design Action Steps

Taking specific, measurable action steps moves the counselee from theory to practice. Action steps can be assigned as homework, reviewed in the subsequent session, and evaluated.

If adjustments need to be made, reassign the action step and repeat the process until there is a measurable result. Be flexible, but be consistent to clearly communicate to the counselee that taking action steps is a critical part of the counseling process. If the counselee wants results, their participation is a primary component. When the counselee fails to do the homework assignments or take any of the steps necessary toward achieving the counseling goals, it may be prudent to suggest that participation in the process is a condition to continue counseling. The counselor's time is valuable and limited. Every counselor must be a good steward of the time and influence God has given him or her in the counseling setting. When the counselee simply wants to complain about their circumstances or have you feel sorry for them, it is counterproductive to effective pastoral counsel and not the best use of the counselor's time.

Communicate Hope

"Hope is informed optimism." — Michael J. Fox[58]

The wise and effective pastoral counselor is a "hope peddler." Communicating hope must be the attitude and expression of the counselor based in God's sovereignty and saving grace. As the counselee learns more about God and the promises in his Word they become equipped to experience the hope there is in a relationship with Jesus. They discover that all they need is found in an all-consuming love affair with the living God. In this relationship is found the motivation for sustainable, life-transforming change.

Listen to and affirm the counselee's feelings of hopelessness, always giving them a reason for hope found in God's promises. Have the counselee look up and write out a promise or promises specific to their sense of hopelessness. When the counselee is unfamiliar with the Bible help them discover Bible study methods that will teach them how to get to better understand God's Word. Take small steps and encourage the counselee to participate in resources available, like classes, seminars, or podcasts.

Practice the Ministry of Presence

Walk with the counselee in their confusion, sorrow or suffering. Practice the ministry of presence. Help the counselee lean into their pain, telling the truth about painful and difficult circumstances in their life and learning to trust God in the process of grieving, healing, and hoping again.

The counselor must be an empathetic listener. Empathy can be described as identifying with another's feelings, whereas sympathy can be described as sharing the feelings of another. When the counselor is empathetic they experience a psychological identification with, or vicarious experience of, the feelings, thoughts, or attitudes of another. Sympathy involves the sharing or another's sorrow or trouble.[59] Empathy permits a distance between counselor and counselee that allows the counselor to stay objective and effective. Sympathy on the other hand can be counter-productive when the counselor's level of feeling or commiseration compromises their ability to be objective.

Do not be seduced by the pain. Maintaining a healthy balance between caring too much and caring too little is a constant challenge for the counselor. Balancing the tension between empathy and sympathy will lead to a healthy expression of compassion. Compassion for another demonstrates the desire to alleviate suffering. This demonstration must be tempered with restraint and built on the authority of God's Word.

Learn healthy boundaries. Never see the counselee outside the confines of the location you have selected to counsel. An exception would be to visit someone who has been incarcerated or hospitalized. Never invite a counselee to live with you. Do not share personal information about where you live, your family's names or your personal telephone number. Resist the temptation to get more involved in the counselee's life than what is required to provide solid biblical counsel. Experience teaches the violation of these guidelines can bring about difficult or disastrous results. Counselees have been known to turn against counselors, their family, or friends perpetrating criminal, litigious, or lascivious behavior. Avoid the risk of this liability at every cost.

Encourage the counselee but do not be their advocate. Stepping outside the boundaries of your role as counselor is not recommended. Trying to advocate where there are social services to provide resources is not a good idea. It is recommended that you become aware of the resources available in your community or region to meet the needs of the counselee, such as medical or dental services, food pantries, or subsidized housing. Be prepared to give the counselee a list of resources.

Do not navigate the system, or negotiate outcomes for them. Never do for the counselee what they must do for themselves. The counselor must maintain healthy boundaries. Learning healthy boundaries equips the counselor to direct the counselee toward God's best, in spite of their pain, confusion, or hopelessness. Remember the moth must beat its wings against the cocoon to build the strength it needs to survive outside its safe enclosure. Keeping healthy boundaries allows the counselee to discover and experience God's best for them.

The counselor must be careful not to demonstrate pity in a manner that cripples the counselee. Pity suggests helplessness.

"Pity is a benign form of abuse." —Michael J. Fox[60]

The counselor must make every effort to help the counselee recognize their capability in Christ. Armed with this awareness, the counselee is more willing to take healthy risks necessary for change. Communicate the truth to the counselee that in Christ all things are possible (Philippians 4:13).

Learn the art of interruption. When the counselee has veered off course and is pursuing a line of thinking that is counter-productive to the counseling process, politely and gently guide them back to the topic at hand. An example would be when the counselee continues to blame another for their circumstances and repeatedly verbalizes their frustration with this person without any willingness to take responsibility for their part in the problem, engage in the counseling process, or work on their relationship with God.

Set the rules of engagement. When the talk style turns to one of anger or the expression of expletives, gently and firmly interrupt the conversation and advise the counselee that this type of talk is inappropriate for the counseling setting. Observing expressions of anger will be helpful and informative in small, measured doses. Avoid allowing repeated outbursts of anger in the counseling session. In the face of such behavior, it may become imperative to recommend anger management classes before counseling continues. As the counselor, set the rules of engagement to ensure the counseling process will be respectful of participants, productive, and God honoring. It is reasonable and acceptable for the counselor to set ground rules that when violated results in the termination of counseling services. Be clear when establishing ground rules that will determine the course of counseling and the consequences should the ground rules be violated.

Questions for Consideration

1. What is the best way to get to know the counselee?
2. How do you establish counseling goals?
3. What is an appropriate action step?

CHAPTER FIVE

Equipping the Counselor to go the Distance

The Fellowship of Suffering

Ministry can be messy. The best way to respond to those who are suffering is to follow the lead of the Master, Jesus Christ. Jesus set the best example for the counselor to follow.

Jesus left glory and entered in to our world. To help people through trauma, tragedy, or grief you must be with them and listen to them. Enter in to their world, join in the fellowship of the suffering, help those God has entrusted to you move toward a new and different place. Ministry to those who hurt is not for the faint of heart.

"You cannot help if you do not enter the darkness."
— Diane Langberg[61]

Be Jesus with skin on. Seldom is it techniques, programs, or plans that transform an individual's experience. Show the counselee God's character through the demonstration of it. People who have experienced loss or trauma need you to hope for them when they cannot hope for themselves.

Jesus did not get lost in the darkness. Jesus entered into darkness, and did not abandon mankind. He not only helps us find our way through the difficult times, he stays by our side as we found our way out.

Remember, when you are going through hell, just keep going. Your words of encouragement can make a difference.

Jesus did not allow the chaos, darkness, or evil, to distract or destroy him. He did not become sin. Jesus entered into the darkness but stayed light.

The Light shines in the darkness, and the darkness did not comprehend it. John 1:5

He entered into the sickness but did not get sick. Every counselor must come to Jesus and drink deeply to endure in carrying living water to dry and thirsty places.

For with You is the fountain of life; in Your light we see light. Psalm 36:9

To be able to bear the burdens of those who come for counsel, the counselor must first be a fit burden-bearer like

Jesus, remembering to do God's work *with* him, *for* him and *through* him.

> *For I have learned in whatever situation I am to be*
> *content. I know how to be brought low, and I know how*
> *to abound. In any and every circumstance, I have learned*
> *the secret of facing plenty and hunger, abundance and*
> *need, I can do all things through him who strengthens me.*
> Philippians 4:11-13 (ESV)

When ministering to the suffering, any barriers between God and the counselor must be removed so that what is done brings glory and honor to him alone.

As discussed in Chapter One, Effective Counsel Begins in the Heart of the Counselor, to go the distance serving in ministry the pastoral counselor must set aside all that hinders. The wise counselor will be intentional in self-awareness, address any strongholds and un-repented sin in their life, and check their motivation for serving.

The counselor who practices good self-care pursues wisdom and commits to life-long learning, refining their skills so they will be a useful tool in God's hand. They maintain a healthy balance in their personal and ministry life, keeping their priorities Christ-centered and God honoring. The individual who goes the distance practices inward, outward, and corporate spiritual disciplines, never allowing lesser pursuits to distract them from spiritual growth and formation.

The Risk of Compassion Fatigue

Those who serve in ministry are at risk for compassion fatigue. Serving as a pastoral counselor presents difficult and challenging situations that expose the counselor to the risk of compassion fatigue. Why be concerned about compassion fatigue?

Compassion fatigue can pose a threat to the spiritual, emotional, and physical wellbeing of the pastoral counselor. It's easy to get caught up in the "doing" of ministry and fail to recognize its impact. Like the "frog in the pot analogy," there is often no realization that the water you're in is boiling. When the realization occurs, the first instinct might be to "jump out," rather than turn down the heat to a manageable degree.

One of the foundational elements of providing effective pastoral care is the realization that we cannot give to others what we ourselves do not possess. When there is a personal lack of spiritual, emotional, and physical wellbeing, the counselor is "running on empty" and has nothing to give to others. In this state, the ability to show compassion to others is compromised and effectiveness of counseling is lost. Effective and efficient care begins with those who live balanced lives demonstrating spiritual, emotional, and physical wellbeing that springs from a heart of spiritual maturity motivated by love for God, self, and others.

Awareness of compassion fatigue equips the individual to serve from the heart, expressing compassion and care.

"The ministry of care must arise from a servant heart—
the heart of compassion and care."[62]

To gain a better understanding of compassion fatigue it is important for the counselor to look at their motivation for serving. Serving from the wrong motivation can cause harm to self and others, putting at risk the helper and those he or she is attempting to help. The right motivation starts with love of God, self, and others. The right motivation is found in response to the Great Commandment (Matthew 22:37, 39).

Another key element in going the distance serving in ministry is to set aside all that keeps individuals from running the race set before them. Those who serve in ministry must set aside every encumbrance and run with endurance.

Lay aside every encumbrance and the sin which so easily entangles us, and let us run with endurance the race that is set before us. Hebrews 12:1

Many things can encumber those who serve from being an effective in tool in God's hands—pride, selfishness, habitual sin, unforgiveness, and anger to name a few. To serve effectively barriers between the counselor and God must be removed. Every counselor must look within and be honest with God, self, and others to be confident these barriers are removed.

A barrier the counselor may not give much thought to is the risk of compassion fatigue. Compassion fatigue poses the risk of keeping individuals from doing the good work God has prepared them to do.

Compassion fatigue encumbers the heart and prevents those who serve from giving effective care. Helping others discover the hope there is in a relationship with Jesus is critical to what the pastoral counselor does. Counseling has the potential to change lives, build God's kingdom, and create a legacy of love. Compassion fatigue prevents this good work from happening.

Working with traumatized individuals can create a demanding and toxic environment, and lead to the experience of negative emotions from anxiety to hopelessness. Learning about compassion fatigue and how to prevent or treat it is about administering the effective antibodies that prevent negative effects, and positively impact the wellbeing of the counselee.

A quote from the CDC sums this idea up:

"Disease is the absence of effective antibodies —
Not the presence of a toxic environment"[63]

Serving in ministry can expose one to a toxic environment. It is important to discover the "effective antibodies" to mitigate the risk of compassion fatigue.

The first step in addressing the risk of compassion fatigue is understanding why it is important to be concerned about the risk of compassion fatigue. The second step is understanding the definition of compassion fatigue and the impact it has on the spiritual, emotional, physical, and psychological well-being of the counselor. The third step is to assess the individual's risk, and the fourth step is learning how to prevent or treat negative effects.

Seeking knowledge, along with the willingness to risk change, equips the counselor with the skills to prevent or mitigate the effects of compassion fatigue.

Charles Figley, a leading expert in the study of compassion fatigue, states that exposure to troubled or traumatized individuals causes secondary traumatic stress for the helper:

"Compassion Fatigue is a natural and disruptive by-product of working with traumatized and troubled clients... it is stress resulting from helping or wanting to help a traumatized person."[64]

Compassion fatigue is sometimes called the "cost of caring." It is a response to exposure to traumatic stress. Serving in ministry sometimes exposes those who serve to individuals who have experienced physical, psychological, or sexual trauma. When this exposure occurs, it can impact the counselor.

"Traumatic events can shatter the sense of connection
between individual and community, creating a crisis
of faith."[65]

When the counselor is exposed to the suffering of others it can shatter the sense of connection between the counselor, the counselee, and even between the counselor and their loved ones. Listening to the horrific stories often shared in the counseling process presents the counselor with the challenge of maintaining a healthy emotional and spiritual balance. Careless, ill-informed, or inappropriate interaction with exposure to traumatic stress presents significant risk for compassion fatigue. The ability to detach effectively from the drama of trauma helps prevent compassion fatigue.

There is a difference between compassion fatigue and burnout:

Burnout: the lack of the ability to "do."

Compassion Fatigue: the lack of ability to "care."

Webster defines burnout as "the exhaustion of physical or emotional strength or motivation, usually as a result of prolonged stress or frustration."[66]

Burnout is the condition that persists even after you've taken a break or rested. Burnout is a condition associated with feelings of hopelessness and difficulties in dealing with work or in doing your job effectively. Compassion fatigue has the characteristics and symptoms of burnout that has progressed to a higher level.[67]

Another important consideration in understanding what compassion fatigue is and how it affects the counselor is to recognize the relationship between the amount of time the counselor spends counseling and the increased risk for compassion fatigue. The number of cumulative hours served by the counselor increases exposure to the risk of compassion fatigue.

It is important for the counselor to establish clear, healthy boundaries. Discover what unique gift or talent they bring to the equation, do this and leave the rest to others. To be a good steward of time and talent, careful attention must be paid to the limits of the counselor's abilities. The counselor must be careful not to identify with their accomplishments or the opinions of others. They must be motivated by their love for God, self, and others. Their commitment of time to counseling must be tempered in the reality of their schedule, life stage, and family priorities.

Self-awareness plays an important part in assessing the risk for compassion fatigue. While training Timothy to serve in ministry, the apostle Paul cautions the young Timothy to exercise self-awareness as he prepares for the work he is about to do. To ensure the ability to go the distance serving in ministry and increase the effectiveness of counsel, the counselor would be wise to pay attention to the advice Paul offered to Timothy

Pay close attention to yourself and to your teaching; persevere in these things, for as you do this you will ensure salvation both for yourself and for those who hear you. 1 Timothy 4:16

Personal growth doesn't happen by accident. Self-awareness must be accompanied by intentionality. The counselor must be "on purpose" in the pursuit of personal growth and wellbeing as they discover their risk for compassion fatigue.

"The formula for developing awareness begins with each individual taking responsibility for their spiritual formation and growth."[68]

Often when those who serve in counseling ministries are exposed to secondary traumatic stress or vicarious traumatization they may entertain the thought that they are not cut out for this kind of work. This may or may not be true, but before discontinuing participation in this worthy cause, evaluate the characteristics of compassion fatigue and consider the possibility that negative effects are causing thoughts that can be mitigated through diligent self-awareness and proper self-care.

Self-awareness includes taking the time needed to pray and reflect. The practice of self-awareness means slowing down enough to recognize any ill effect the symptoms of compassion fatigue are having on one's ability to counsel and more importantly, on their relationships. Check in with loved ones and inquire about their observations; they may have a better perspective.

One of the key characteristics of compassion fatigue that manifests in a negative emotional response is described as a lack of empathy. The ability to share in another's feelings may become compromised as the symptoms of compassion fatigue start to manifest in the counselor's life. Empathy is a critical component of pastoral counseling. Being fully engaged in the counseling process exposes the counselor to the challenge of caring in a balanced manner that ministers to the counselee but does not harm the counselor. Deep sympathy and sorrow can take a toll. Maintaining a healthy balance presents challenges to those who serve that must be routinely monitored. To maintain balance, self-awareness must be partnered with recognition of the characteristics of compassion fatigue.

Discovering how the symptoms of secondary traumatic stress impact the individual is helpful to assessing the risk of compassion fatigue. The symptoms are described below.

The Personal Impact of Secondary Traumatic Stress [69]

Cognitive	Emotional	Behavioral
• Diminished concentration	• Powerlessness	• Clingy
• Confusion	• Anxiety	• Impatient
• Spaciness	• Guilt	• Irritable
• Loss of meaning	• Anger/rage	• Withdrawn
• Decreased self-esteem	• Survivor guilt	• Moody
• Preoccupation with trauma	• Shutdown	• Regression
• Trauma imagery	• Numbness	• Sleep disturbances
• Apathy	• Fear	• Appetite changes
• Rigidity	• Helplessness	• Nightmares
• Disorientation	• Sadness	• Hypervigilance
• Whirling thoughts	• Depression	• Elevated startle response
• Thoughts of self-harm or harm toward others	• Hypersensitivity	• Use of negative coping (smoking, alcohol, or other substance abuse)
• Self-doubt	• Emotional roller coaster	• Accident proneness
• Perfectionism	• Overwhelmed	• Losing things
• Minimization	• Depleted	• Self-harm behaviors

continued

Spiritual	Interpersonal	Physical
• Questioning the meaning of life • Loss of purpose • Lack of self-satisfaction • Pervasive hopelessness • Ennui (weariness)	• Withdrawn • Decreased interest in intimacy or sex • Mistrust • Isolation from friends • Impact on parenting (protectiveness, concern about aggression) • Projection of anger or blame • Intolerance • Loneliness	• Shock • Sweating • Rapid heartbeat • Breathing difficulties • Somatic (of the body) reactions • Aches and pains • Dizziness • Impaired immune system

When the counselor recognizes symptoms of compassion fatigue in their life they must be wise and discerning to understand if these symptoms are related to compassion fatigue or are a result of issues in their life such as illness, loss, or stress. It is recommended that the counselor carefully review the symptoms they may be experiencing with a trusted advisor to clearly recognize which symptoms might be relative to compassion fatigue and which symptoms are resulting from other life events. Self-awareness serves as an effective tool in recognizing symptoms, assessing the risk for compassion fatigue, and maintaining balance and wellbeing.

There are tools available to help assess the risk of compassion fatigue. The Professional Quality of Life Scale (PROQOL)

Compassion Satisfaction and Compassion Fatigue Version 5 (2009)[70] is one of many tools available. The ProQOL Version 5 a good measurement tool for pastoral counselors to use because of the questions asked and the method of scoring. The ProQOL Version 5 assessment tool has thirty questions designed to measure compassion satisfaction, burnout and secondary traumatic stress (compassion fatigue). Because the test is designed for professional caregivers, a few of the questions may not apply to the pastoral counselor.

As the counselor gains a better understanding of the definition of compassion fatigue, recognizes its characteristics and symptoms, and assesses the risk, the next step will be to prevent or address compassion fatigue.

To prevent or mitigate compassion fatigue, the practice of good self-care is critical. The Psalmist reminds and encourages the reader to "cease striving" and know God (Psalm 46:10).

The Message translation of Matthew 11:29 uses the phrase, "Learn the unforced rhythms of grace."[71] The counselor who adopts the practice of good self-care and complete reliance on God guards against the risk of compassion fatigue and becomes equipped to go the distance in ministry with the ease and synergy found in the "unforced rhythms of grace."

Vulnerability to compassion fatigue is often due to the depletion of the counselor's resources. This condition may prevent the counselor from preserving a critical distance between themselves and the events being related by the counselee. Exposure to the retelling of traumatic events can cause secondary stress, which poses a threat to the counselor's well-being. God gives each individual what is needed to live out the practice of self-care. In complete reliance on the Holy Spirit is found the strength to make the choice to develop the healthy habits necessary to prevent compassion fatigue.

Jesus modeled the discipline of self-care. The practice of good self-care is built on the solid foundation of God's Word. Self-care built on the foundation of God's Word sustains the effort and personal discipline necessary to go the distance and live out the practice in the day-to-day.

Counselors must give themselves permission to laugh, rest, and play, practicing what John Maxwell calls the "Law of Consistency," moving beyond the decision to change habits to the discipline of doing so.

Experts in burnout and compassion fatigue caution the caregiver to make self-care a regular practice. Practicing the discipline of self-care enables those who serve to avoid the risk of compassion fatigue. The counselor must be intentional in this practice to ensure good result, experiencing "intentional growth" as opposed to "accidental growth."[72] Good self-care allows the individual to run the race with endurance and to finish well without losing heart or growing weary. When Jesus says "learn from me," he provides examples of what good self-care looks like. The wise counselor follows the lead of the master.

Jesus modeled rest and solitude in his ministry. Jesus was careful to take the time needed to reflect and restore. Throughout the gospels we find examples of Jesus getting away from the crowd, even from the apostles, to spend time with his Father.

Jesus modeled the practice of solitude often. While preparing for his ministry he spent forty days alone in the desert (Matthew 4:1-11). Before choosing the twelve apostles he spent an entire night alone in the hills (Luke 6:12). Upon hearing of the death of John the Baptist he withdrew to a lonely place (Matthew 14:13). And, after the feeding of the five thousand, he went to the hills for some time to himself (Matthew 14:23).

The definition for self-care is unique to the individual. Each person must discover what recharges his or her batteries. When the counselor adopts the discipline of good self-care it guards against the risk of compassion fatigue.

Relative to spiritual wellbeing, good self-care involves the practice of spiritual disciplines. Consider adding a new spiritual discipline to your spiritual habits. A fuller discussion of the practice of spiritual disciplines is in Chapter 1.

The inward disciplines of meditation, prayer, fasting, and study take the individual to the deepest and highest work of the human spirit. The outward disciplines of simplicity, solitude, submission, and service are demonstrated in full surrender to the authority of God's Word and absolute surrender to his will. The corporate disciplines of confession, worship, guidance, and celebration must become regular habits.

A joyful heart is good medicine. Proverbs 17:22

There is a connection between humor and a positive state of mind. "Humor's most important psychological function is to jolt us out of our habitual frame of mind and promote new perspectives."[73] Lighten the burden of counseling with fun and frivolous things. Try not to spend too much time in a serious mood; instead, enjoy a "serious dose of silly" on a regular basis. It does the body, mind, and soul good.

As discussed in Chapter One, motivation for serving must come from pure intentions, from a selfless rather than selfish desire to care for another. Right motivation springs from the belief that we must love our neighbor as ourselves. Serving from incorrect motives can harm those you are trying to help as well as yourself.

"True service comes from a relationship with the divine Other deep inside. Self-righteous service requires external rewards. It needs to know that people see and appreciate the effort. True service rests contented in hiddenness."[74]

The practice of self-care includes recognizing your limitations. Setting healthy boundaries and sticking to them helps ensure a balanced schedule. It is recommended the counselor have an accountability partner to assist in this endeavor.

It is also critical the counselor know their shape and season for ministry to ensure they are serving from their giftedness and being a good steward of their time and resources.

There is an appointed time for everything. And there is a time for every event under heaven. Ecclesiastes 3:1

To practice good self-care in the area of physical well-being requires diligence and consistency. Most don't need to be reminded of the benefits of maintaining a healthy diet, getting proper rest, and regular exercise. Jesus modeled these good habits of self-care...snack and a nap...it's biblical!

Proper exercise can increase energy, boost the immune system, reduce stress, and even decrease irritability. Getting the proper amount of rest boosts the immune system and provides optimal energy.

My son, give attention to my words; incline your ear to my sayings. Do not let them depart from your sight; keep them in the midst of your heart. For they are life to those who find them and health to all their body.
Proverbs 4:20–22

Coping strategies to address the psychological symptoms of compassion fatigue include having a positive support system. A positive support system can provide opportunities to discuss such delicate topics as the continuum of mental illness, mandated reporting, or suicide assessment. It can also provide a confidential setting to process emotions and gain perspective. It is an opportunity to ask for prayer to acquire insight and wisdom from others in the group. Form a group with others in the counseling ministry who are trained and adherent to confidentiality.

Ten Suggestions for Self-care

1. Start a journal—use the journal to process your feelings.
2. Reflect on your own history—why do you serve in this area?
3. Reexamine your motives—what are your motivations for serving in this area?
4. Nourish and replenish yourself—what recharges your batteries?
5. Think about your strengths and values—are they helpful in your service?
6. Deal with your energizers and drainers—What type of experience fills you up, what type drains you?
7. Deal with overextending and overwork—don't take on more than you can handle. Learn how to say "no."
8. Watch for signs of burnout—including emotional withdrawal, avoidance of intimacy, feelings of helplessness and sleep disturbances.
9. Consider seeking counsel for yourself.
10. Practice spiritual disciplines:
    a. Inward disciplines: meditation, prayer, fasting, and study.
    b. Outward disciplines: simplicity, solitude, submission, and service.
    c. Corporate disciplines: confession, worship, guidance, and celebration.

Therefore everyone who hears these words of Mine and acts on them, may be compared to a wise man who built his house on the rock. Matthew 7:24

Questions for Consideration.

1. What is the difference between burnout and compassion fatigue?
2. Why is it important to understand what compassion fatigue is and how it impacts the pastoral counselor?
3. List three ways to prevent compassion fatigue.

CHAPTER SIX

Practical Considerations

Liability Insurance

"California courts imposed a legal duty on psychotherapists to warn third parties of patients' threats to their safety in 1976 in Tarasoff v. The Regents of the University of California."[75] This law established a legal precedent exposing the pastoral counselor to the risk of lawsuit. It is advisable to secure liability insurance, available through various professional associations and agencies to protect against lawsuits.

Seek professional advice and learn about confidentiality and the law as well as your exposure to liability. Review the penal code for your state or region on Mandatory Reporting Laws so that you know when confidentiality must be broken and an offense must be reported.

Confidentiality

Confidentiality is critical to the ministry of counseling. Every effort must be taken on the part of the counselor to protect the confidentiality of the counseling relationship. The only exceptions are covered in the following section on Mandated Reporting. The exceptions to confidentiality occur rarely.

To protect the counselee, and the witness of the ministry, the church and the gospel it is important that information about the counselee not be shared with anyone outside the immediate counseling ministry. When the counselee is not confident the counselor will keep information shared confidential they are not be willing to develop a relationship of trust with the counselor. Disclose in the first session the areas where confidentiality must be broken. Have the counselee sign an agreement that states they understand Mandated Reporting and your responsibility as a counselor.

In larger church settings where the counseling ministry is an entity of its own counselors are encouraged not to share any information with church staff members, friends or family. In some cases, even the senior pastor. The size and dynamic of your church helps in determining the scope of confidentiality. A clear understanding of the mandated reporting laws also helps determine the boundaries necessary to protect the ministry.

Within the ministry, when there are supervision groups the counselors attend regularly it is imperative the counselor give as few details as possible about the counselee's identity when seeking advice from other counselors. In this setting the counselor may refer to their counselee in non-descriptive terms.

Mandated Reporting

Areas where confidentiality is waived or limited are: suicide, child abuse, elder and dependent adult abuse, and homicidal threats.

A religious practitioner, or similar functionary of a church, including church staff and volunteers, are mandated reporters while performing church duties. Should they have reasonable suspicion that abuse has taken place the report is to be made immediately by phone and followed up by a written report to the same agency within 36 hours. The initial report is made to the appropriate legal agency immediately or as soon as is practicably possible by telephone and the mandated reporter shall prepare and send, fax, or electronically transmit a written follow up report thereof within 36 hours of receiving the information concerning the incident. It is critical that the pastoral counselor know the law for the jurisdiction in which they serve. Failure to make an abuse report is punishable by law and subject to a fine. If the pastoral counselor is uncertain or has reasonable doubt about an offense it is wise to seek counsel from the pastor overseeing the ministry. The responsibility to report still falls to the pastoral counselor who received the information.

A report filed on the basis of suicidal threat is made once the counselor has assessed the counselee and determined the threat is real and imminent. If the counselee is unwilling to take steps recommended by the counselor for their safety it is imperative that a report be made to the proper authorities to ensure the counselee's safety and wellbeing.

The reporting law is comprehensive as to what constitutes child abuse or neglect. A child is considered anyone under the age of eighteen years. Abuse can be physical, sexual or psychological. Physical abuse includes any cruel or inhuman corporal punishment or injury resulting in a traumatic condition.

Neglect can take the form of failure to provide medical, physical or educational necessities, including malnutrition or exposure to dangerous circumstances.

Sexual abuse includes any inappropriate touching of genitalia, performance of any sex act or sexual exploitation including photos or exposure to pornography. For a full list of details see your state's penal code.

An elder is considered to be a person over the age of 65. Elder abuse includes punching, hitting, kicking or otherwise inflicting bodily injury. Neglect includes failure to provide safety, nutrition or hygiene. Financial abuse is also a reportable event.

A dependent adult is a person over the age of 18 who is dependent on another for basic needs due to illness, injury or disability. Dependent adult abuse includes inflicting bodily injury, unreasonable restraint, or failure to provide nutritional and medical necessities.

A homicidal threat occurs when a statement is made about inflicting bodily harm against an individual or group. This threat is viable when the individual making the threat is serious in their intent and has a plan to carry it out.

It is always advised to err on the side of caution, choosing to report rather than to fail to protect an individual or group. When there is reasonable suspicion a report must be made. When there is uncertainty, consult an authority. Reasonable suspicion is defined as, "Would a reasonable person, one who is objective, based on the facts, have cause to suspect that abuse, neglect or threat has taken place?"

Location

Location for counseling is critical. Counsel in a location that provides both confidentiality and visibility.

Make every effort to protect the ministry, the individuals involved and the church where you serve. Choose a location that is private so that the counselee feels comfortable. An office with a door is preferable as this way no one can listen in thus violating the privacy of the counselee. An office with a window or glass door is also preferable, as this will help prevent any appearance of impropriety. It is recommended that counseling occur in a location and timeframe when others will be present. This ensures protection for the counselor as well as the counselee.

Security is also a consideration for the counseling setting. To ensure the safety of both the counselor and the counselee it is wise to have security personnel on the premises during counseling hours. The size of the church where you serve sometimes determines if this is feasible. Larger churches often have security personnel on the payroll. There is always a possibility that the counselor or counselee will be at risk, so do all that is necessary to provide a secure counseling setting. In cases where the counselee has a restraining order be sure to uphold the law, never making exceptions without court approval, to violate a restraining order. A counselee might have a false sense of security, indicating that their loved one has repented and changed their ways. Without the proper legal documentation never violate a restraining order based on what the counselee tells you. Ask for written documentation to support statements made by the counselee. When a counselee shows up in violation of an existing restraining order immediately discontinue the counseling session, call authorities if necessary and ensure the safety of the counselee without putting yourself at risk.

Scheduling

It is important to find a scheduling system. A scheduling system can be as simple as a notebook or as complex as a custom-designed digital solution. Depending on the size of the counseling ministry scheduling systems can be as robust or as simple as indicated to properly manage the counselor's as well as the counselee's schedules. Digital systems used in medical practices are available and often provide the measure of confidentiality necessary to manage counseling appointments.

It is also very helpful to have a system that automatically sends reminders to both the counselor and counselee of their appointed time. Custom scheduling systems and some off-the-shelf programs can be costly. Take the time needed to do the research into which program is best for your ministry.

File Management

To ensure proper file management, it is recommended that counselors have a file folder for each counselee with the appropriate forms and notes from meetings secured inside. These files should never leave the counseling area or be left unattended in the counselor's workspace to ensure confidentiality.

Provide each counselor with intake forms designed to gather detailed information about the counselee's name, address, phone number, emergency contact and medical information. These forms should be filled out during the first session along with a statement from the counselor as to the nature of the counseling ministry, confidentiality, and when confidentiality must be broken. Explain to the counselee the areas where confidentiality must be broken as indicated by the laws governing mandated reporting such as threat of suicide, child, elder or dependent adult abuse or threat of homicide. Go over the information with the counselee during the first session and answer any questions they might have. The counselor and the counselee then sign and date the two statements. One copy is given to the counselee the other stays in the counselee's folder.

It is critical to keep the counselee's file folder in a secure location to prevent any violation of confidentiality. Do not share information from the folder with family members, staff or others who might inquire about the status of counseling. Never surrender the file to authorities without the proper legal procedure such as a search warrant. Even a subpoena can be challenged by the legal system. Consult a legal authority to learn your responsibility and legal obligation in this matter.

CHAPTER SEVEN

Conclusion

B e encouraged, and steadfast in the good work you are
doing. Speak against the sense of amorality that is shaping
a worldview of uncommon decency. Embrace both the privilege and the responsibility to address the moral dilemmas challenging many today. Walk with those in crisis and help them
develop a sense of morality shaped by biblical authority rather
than cultural influence.

Pastoral counseling done from the proper perspective,
authority, and motivation has the power to transform lives.
Effective pastoral counseling brings healing to those who
hurt, guidance to those who are lost, and hope to the hopeless.
Pastoral counseling done in the authority of God's Word and
direction of the Holy Spirit provides light for the way to those
willing to obey biblical principles.

*Let us not lose heart in doing good, for in due time we
will reap if we do not grow weary.* Galatians 6:9

Review

- Remember that effective counseling begins in the heart of the counselor.
- Be committed to spiritual formation and life-long learning and the practice of good self-care.
- Understand the two primary goals of counseling are discipleship and evangelism.
- God's Word is the authority in counseling.
- Be willing to set aside the behaviors, attitudes, or practices that hinder you.
- Be intentional in understanding the risk of compassion fatigue.
- Be persistent in preventing or mitigating the symptoms of compassion fatigue.
- Be accountable to someone for the positive changes you are willing to make as you address the risk of compassion fatigue.
- Keep an attitude of gratitude.

For God has not given us a spirit of timidity, but of power and love and discipline. 2 Timothy 1:7

About the Author

After studying fine art at Cal State University Long Beach Kathy enjoyed a lengthy career as a graphic designer in the advertising industry. In 2004 Kathy was invited to join the Pastoral Care Team at Saddleback Church in Lake Forest, California where she was licensed to ministry and served as Minister of Counseling for twelve years. Kathy counseled individuals and couples from church staff, church membership and the community. She shared responsibility for the care and discipleship of more than two hundred and fifty volunteer church counselors serving in the Church Counseling Ministry. She taught a thirty-week Church Counseling Training course, and wrote devotionals and curriculum for counselor advanced training to encourage, equip and edify those serving in ministry. Currently, she enjoys an international presence as a speaker, writer and teacher.

Kathy has a Bachelor of Science in Organizational Leadership from Biola University, a Master of Arts in Theological Study from Golden Gate Baptist Theological Seminary, and a Doctorate in Ministry from Golden Gate Baptist Theological Seminary (Gateway).

Kathy has written a 20-hour curriculum designed to train individual counselors to serve in pastoral counseling ministry. She is founder of Hope Connection and a sought-after retreat, workshop and event speaker.

Endnotes

1   Naomi K. Paget and Janet R. McCormack, *The Work of the Chaplain* (Valley Forge, PA: Judson Press, 2006), 23.

2   John Maxwell. *The 15 Invaluable Laws of Growth* (New York: Center Street a division of Hachette Book Group Inc., 2012), 29.

3   Richard J. Foster. *The Celebration of Discipline: The Path to Spiritual Growth* (New York: Harper Collins Publishers, 1998), 1.

4   Bernie S. Siegel, *Love, Medicine & Miracles* (New York: HarperCollins Publishers, 1986), 145.

5   Erik Rees, *S.H.A.P.E.: Finding and Fulfilling Your Unique Purpose for Life* (Grand Rapids: Zondervan, 2006), 24.

6   Priscilla Shirer, *Discerning the Voice of God: How to Recognize When God is Speaking* (Chicago: Moody Publishers, 2012), 61.

7   David B. Guralnik, Editor, *Webster's New World Dictionary of the American Language* (New York: Prentice Hall Press, A Division of Simon & Schuster, Inc., 1986), 732.

8   Andrew Murray, *Humility: Beauty of Holiness* (Lexington: Fig-Books, 2010), 47.

9   Andrew Murray, *Absolute Surrender* (Lamp Post Inc., 2009), 59.

10 Tim Harlow, *Life on Mission: God's People Finding God's Heart for the World* (Rancho Santa Margarita: Pastors.com, 2014), 149.

11 Tim Harlow, *Life on Mission: God's People Finding God's Heart for the World* (Rancho Santa Margarita: Pastors.com, 2014), 194.

12 Hugh F. Halverstadt, *Managing Church Conflict* (Louisville: Westminster/John Knox Press, 1991), 26.

13 Hugh F. Halverstadt, *Managing Church Conflict* (Louisville: Westminster/John Knox Press, 1991), 25, 37.

14 Reggie Thomas, "Conflict Management in Ministry" (lecture on Forgiveness, Golden Gate Baptist Theological Seminary, Brea, CA, October 31, 2012).

15 Ken Sande, *The Peacemaker*. (Grand Rapids: Baker Books, 2004), 208.

16 23. Viktor E. Frankl, *Man's Search for Meaning*. (Massachusetts: Beacon Press, 1959), xi.

17 Bernie S. Siegel, M.D., *Love, Medicine & Miracles*. (New York: Harper & Rowe, Publishers, Inc., 1986), 192.

18 Roy T. Denton & Michael W. Martin, *Defining Forgiveness: An Empirical Exploration of Process and Role the American Journal of Family Therapy*. (New York: Brunner-Mazel Publishing Company, 1998), 282, 288.

19 5. Erich Fromm. *The Heart of Man: It's Genius for Good and Evil*. (New York: Harper & Brothers, 1956), 173–178.

20 Ken Sande, *The Peacemaker*. (Grand Rapids: Baker Books, 2004), 206.

21 Barna, "New Marriage and Divorce Statistics." www. barna.com.

22 Shaunti Feldhahn, *The Surprising Secrets of Highly Happy Marriages: The Little Things That Make a Big Difference* (Colorado Springs: Multnomah, 2013), 178.

23 Barry Lord, Domestic Violence Training, San Diego, CA, 2012.

24 www.family.findlaw.com/domestic-violence. Accessed online 2012.

25 Millard Erickson. *Christian Theology, Second Edition* (Grand Rapids: Baker Books, 2013), 474.

26 Francis Frangipani, *The Three Battlegrounds* (Cedar Rapids: Arrow Publications, Inc., 1989), 34.

27 Barna Group, Barna Trends 2017 *What's New and What's Next at the Intersection of Faith and Culture* (Grand Rapids: Baker Books, 2017), 53.

28 Mark A. Yarhouse, *Understanding Gender Dysphoria Navigating Transgender Issues in a Changing Culture* (Downers Grove: InterVarsity Press, 2015), 17, 20.

29 American Psychiatric Association, *Diagnostic and Statistical Manual of Mental Disorders, 5th ed.* (Washington, DC: American Psychiatric Publishing, 2013), 451–459.

30 Mark A. Yarhouse, *Understanding Gender Dysphoria Navigating Transgender Issues in a Changing Culture* (Downers Grove: InterVarsity Press, 2015), 24.

31 Barna Group, Barna Trends 2017 *What's New and What's Next at the Intersection of Faith and Culture* (Grand Rapids: Baker Books, 2017), 173.

32 Ted Roberts, The Neurochemistry of Addiction, Pure desire Ministries www.puredesire.org.

33 Barna Group, Barna Trends 2017, *What's New and What's Next at the Intersection of Faith and Culture* (Grand Rapids: Baker Books, 2017), 100.

34 Barna Group, Barna Trends 2017, *What's New and What's Next at the Intersection of Faith and Culture* (Grand Rapids: Baker Books, 2017), 50.

35 Barna Group, *Barna Trends 2017*, 98.

36 http://www.nami.org/ Accessed 06/24/2013.

37 Christianity Today, *Can Prayer and Bible Study Overcome Mental Illness?* (Carol Stream: Christianity Today, November, 2013), 23.

38 American Psychiatric Association, *Diagnostic and Statistical Manual of Mental Disorders, 4th ed.* (Washington, DC: American Psychiatric Publishing, 2000), 349.

39 American Psychiatric Association, *Diagnostic and Statistical Manual of Mental Disorders, 5th ed.* (Washington, DC: American Psychiatric Publishing, 2013), 349.

40 American Psychiatric Association, *Diagnostic and Statistical Manual of Mental Disorders, 4th ed.* (Washington, DC: American Psychiatric Publishing, 2000), 298–302.

41 American Psychiatric Association, *Diagnostic and Statistical Manual of Mental Disorders, 4th ed.* (Washington, DC: American Psychiatric Publishing, 2000), 425.

42 American Psychiatric Association, *Diagnostic and Statistical Manual of Mental Disorders*, 4th ed. 443.

43 http://www.mayoclinic.org/diseases-conditions/narcissistic-personality-disorder/basics/definition/con-20025568

44 Michael J. Fox, *The Kid's Alright*, AARP The Magazine, April/May 2017 (New York: AARP The Magazine, 2017), 54.

45 Orange County Register (Santa Ana: Division of Digital First Media, November 29, 2015).

46 http://medicalxpress.com/news/2010-04-children-parent-suicide-die.html. Accessed 11/14/16.

47 David B. Guralnik, Editor in Chief, *Webster's New World Dictionary of the American Language*. (New York: Prentice Hall Press A Division of Simon & Schuster, Inc., 1986), 1513.

48 48. Judith Lewis Herman, *Trauma and Recovery* (New York: Basic Books 1997), 55.

49 Diane Langberg, *Suffering and The Heart of God, How Trauma Destroys and Christ Restores*. (Greensborough: New Growth Press, 2015), 5.

50 John Piper, *When the Darkness Will Not Lift: Doing What We Can While We Wait for God—and Joy* (Wheaton: Crossway Books, 2006), 42.

51 Brennan Manning, *The Furious Longing of God*. (Colorado Springs: David C. Cook, 2009), 24.

52 Elisabeth Kübler-Ross, *On Grief and Grieving: Finding the Meaning of Grief Through the Five Stages of Loss*. (New York: Scribner, 2005.)

53 Jerry Sittser, *A Grace Revealed: How God Redeems the Story of Your Life*, (Grand Rapids: Zondervan, 2012), 13, 15, 147.

54 Richard J. Foster, *Celebration of Discipline: The Path to Spiritual Growth*

(New York: HarperCollins Publishers, 1998), 1.

55 Andrew Murray, *Absolute Surrender* (Lamp Post Inc., 2009), 59.

56 http://www.myersbriggs.org/ Meyers & Briggs Personality Test 16. Accessed online 06/20/17.

57 Gary Chapman, *The 5 Love Languages: The Secret to Love that Lasts, New Edition* (Chicago: Northfield Publishing, 2015.)

58 Michael J. Fox, *The Kid's Alright*, AARP The Magazine, April/May 2017 (New York: AARP The Magazine, 2017), 54.

59 www.dictionary.com

60 Michael J. Fox, Orange County Register, Parade Section 04/01/12

61 Diane Langberg, *Suffering and the Heart of God: How Trauma Destroys and Christ Restores* (Greensborough: New Growth Press, 2015), 113.

62 Naomi K. Paget and Janet R. McCormack, *The Work of the Chaplain* (Valley Forge, PA: Judson Press, 2006), 23.

63 J. Eric Gentry, *Compassion Fatigue Prevention and Resiliency: Professional Motivation* (GONL 2012, The Courage to Lead) Transcript, PG 10, programs.gha.org, accessed May 15, 2014.

64 Charles R. Figley, Ph.D. *Compassion Fatigue: Coping with Secondary Traumatic Stress Disorder in Those Who Treat the Traumatized* (New York: Routledge, 1995), xiv.

65 Judith Lewis Herman, M.D., *Trauma and Recovery* (New York: Basic Books 1997), 55.

66 David B. Guralnik, Editor in Chief. *Webster's New World Dictionary of the American Language.* (New York: Prentice Hall Press, 1986), 190.

67 Christine Florio, *Burnout and Compassion Fatigue: A Guide for Mental Health Professionals and Care Givers* (San Bernardino: CreateSpace 2010), 7.

68 John Maxwell. *The 15 Invaluable Laws of Growth: Live Them and Reach Your Potential* (New York: Center Street, a division of Hachette Book Group Inc., 2012), 29.

69 Charles R. Figley, ed, *Compassion Fatigue: Coping with Secondary Traumatic Stress Disorder in Those Who Treat the Traumatized* (New York: Routledge, an imprint of Taylor and Francis Group 1995), 184.

70 © B. Hudnall Stamm, 2009-2012. *Professional Quality of Life: Compassion Satisfaction and Fatigue Version 5* (ProQOL), www.proqol.org.

71 *Contemporary Comparative Side-by-Side Bible: New International Version and New King James Version and New Living Translation and The Message* (Grand Rapids: Zondervan, 1984), 2271.

72 John Maxwell. *The 15 Invaluable Laws of Growth* (New York: Center Street Hachette Book Group, 2012), 13.

73 Bernie S. Siegel, *Love, Medicine & Miracles* (New York: HarperCollins, 1986), 145.

74 Foster. Ibid. 128.

75 www.ncsl.org. Accessed 06/2017.

CPSIA information can be obtained
at www.ICGtesting.com
Printed in the USA
FSHW021743260219
55953FS

9 781545 657515